GROWING GUARDIANS, TRAINING SHEEPDOGS

Using Human-centered, Principle-Based Police Training

MARC NEAL

ONYX TRAINING LTD

ISBN:978-1-7366609-1-1 Print version
ISBN:978-1-7366609-0-4 E Book

Cover design by Julie Brookins/Marc Neal
Printed in the United States of America

Dedicated to the flock,

And

the Sheepdogs who protect us.

Contents

Preface

If I must nail down the exact moment I decided to write this book it would have to be after the second young officer made a really disturbing comment during one of my basic SWAT classes. He was only the second one in 15 years, but the comment showed such disregard for his role as a police officer, let alone an advanced tactics operator, that I knew I must write this book.

I show a specific video of an elderly lady swaying and dancing in a driveway next to a road. It is a suburban area, no houses visible to the road in the video. Just trees, shrubs, etc.

There is a police officer kneeling behind a bush about 25 feet from the lady. She appears to not notice him; at least she pays him no attention. She doesn't appear to be angry or mad. She is dancing!

In one hand she holds an old school cordless phone, complete with antennae. In the other, a revolver. The clip I use is the last two minutes of an event that lasted almost an hour.

As this lady dances and sways, she raises the gun much in the way she would do if she were casting a fishing pole. The barrel swings up in the air in an arc, then comes to a not quite level position, pointed away from her. Not at all a serious effort to aim by any stretch.

She gets shot from off camera. One round. She falls down, dropping both phone and revolver.

Three officers rush up to her, one kicks the gun away from her. She's not thinking about going for it, trust me. A second officer attempts to reholster his weapon but can't seem to find the holster. This is significant.

A third officer, the one who was kneeling, runs up holding his gun on her. The officers all appear to be having trouble processing what just happened.

I show this video to begin our less lethal section lecture, so you may understand where I am going with this.

This is when I ask the class their thoughts about the chosen use of force. Usually, I get some halfhearted excuse that she pointed the gun at an officer. They try to justify an action that deep inside them they don't feel is justified. Or at least an action they realize is not the most desired thing to do.

I come back at them with something about her lack of aim, her non-threatening demeanor, her actual level of threat to any officer smart enough to be behind cover (something that would stop the bullets).

Any officer shot by this lady should have only themselves to blame.

In today's police training we seem to be teaching our officers to shoot first and ask questions later, so I am looking to see how they rank and justify threats. I train officers to respond to known threats, not hypotheticals, so I am always interested to know what officers around the country are being taught.

Usually, the students then acknowledge the reality of the situation and understand that to simply shoot this lady is not in the best interests of their oath to "to protect and serve". Usually.

Once in a while I get a determined one. These officers believe that they are the most important person in the world because their mom said so, and they don't care who points a gun or where it's pointed, that person is getting shot.

I increase the emotional connection by saying this lady is their grandmother. She has early onset dementia or Alzheimer's, and she is not in her cogent mind. Or maybe she is drunk because her husband of 60 years has recently passed away and she is not sure how she is going to get through the rest of her life without him. I want them to see this lady as someone's family.

I want them to see her as a fellow human being.

This usually brings around the .1% to an understanding that we have an obligation to go above and beyond just waiting for a chance to shoot. *Usually.*

One day in class, a student said, "Well I guess its grandma's day to die."

He said it so matter of fact, so nonchalant, like he had already thought about this very scenario, and didn't really much care for his grandma. His teammate, seated next to him in the class, physically leaned away from him, because lightening. The entire class let out an audible "WTF?!"

Even during a poignant, truly articulate, well-substantiated discussion, he would not or could not change his mind.

He felt it was more acceptable that an officer too dumb to stand behind a house or a wall be able to kill his dementia-addled or grieving grandmother, than be expected to use any of the plethora of chemical, flash sound, or extended range impact less lethal resources or tools available to civilian law enforcement today. His grandma gave him too many bad birthday presents, I guess.

The *second* time, a student said it was "too bad, I'm going home."

Such a short, simple three-word sentence and resulting mentality that I think has contributed to a majority of the tragedies that have ripped open this chasm of distrust and fear between growing segments of the public and law enforcement. The declaration, "I go home." seems so sensible and obvious on its own.

However, taken in the overall context of police activity, our role, our duties, and oath of office, it promotes a rigid mindset where fluidity is required. It creates contradiction where we need consistency.

When a police officer says that sentence, "I go home" or an agency instills that mindset in their new officers, they establish a mentality that considers self-preservation first and foremost. A law enforcement officer must put their lives on the line in certain circumstances. But if we teach and preach "I go home", officers will default to that every time.

In the response from these two officers, and others, I realized some significant dynamics at play. I noticed a disturbing absence of empathy for strangers, and a lack of empathy period.

Coming from my own perspective it would have been easy for me to dismiss and ridicule these young officers' views and beliefs. It would have been easy for me to discount them as dumb, idiots, or even racists, as some people might call them in certain instances.

But in reality, both officers, and all law enforcement officers, view the world from the only perspective they can. A perspective based on their experiences, held beliefs, and what they have been taught about *everything,* including police tactics. This singular, selfish perspective applies to people in general.

It was then that I realized we are teaching our police officers to shoot Alzheimer's patients, mental health patients, drunk people, and others simply because we have hammered into them the wonderfully myopic mantra "I go home." We aren't giving them the tools and knowledge to do anything else.

We are creating police officers who do not consider other people as having equal human value to themselves.

Our society's innate, ingrained senses of hierarchy, bias, "different equals bad", combined with police mindset training of self-preservation above all else, have led to profound decision-making problems in policing.

It is no wonder why officers will shoot an unarmed man walking towards them holding a cell phone. Or why they would shoot a man sitting in his car reaching for his wallet as requested, while his daughter sat directly behind him.

I want to encourage a paradigm shift for myself, for other trainers, and for law enforcement as a whole. The movement is to create, develop, and encourage a new type of police training.

This shift will focus on confidence building principles and tactics. It will develop Guardians, considerate and understanding of their role in the community.

This book is the start of a movement.

I am on a mission to restore and repair the relationship between the community and law enforcement. And I am doing it by presenting high quality police training. My goal with this book is to start a revolution of reconnection and improved relationships.

I am certain that the information and knowledge I prescribe will accomplish what all groups want. Police officers will increase the odds that they will get to "go home". Police agencies will have well trained, liability reducing, competent police officers.

Most important, communities will have truly trustworthy, committed Guardians who understand the interdependent partnership between law enforcement and the communities it serves.

This book is not intended solely for law enforcement eyes. It contains nothing secret. There are no special ninja tactics explained so the suspect can know our secrets.

I want the general public to read this book and realize the information in it will not only help law enforcement but will make the public safer too. I want the public to understand where the deficiency lies and realize it can be cured.

But like any sickness, we need a restorative and therapeutic approach to healing. This will take the efforts of everyone, together.

Community-affecting illnesses need community-invested remedies.

The most important thing to me is for policing to be seen in the light it deserves. Law enforcement is the most noble profession. I believe in it and the people who choose to be a part of it. I have nothing but support for good police officers who take on the role of protectors of their communities.

The Low COP (Lowrider Community Outreach Program). A grant and donation-based project I created when I was a police officer.

Introduction

"Do We Really Need to Shoot Grandma?"

A growing number of citizens are calling for the defunding and abolishment of the policing system as it exists now. People are now more scared of police than they are of criminals. The citizens have lost trust in the word of police officers, and sadly, for legitimate reason.

There are too many tragedies where law enforcements officers have killed, injured, or simply verbally abused innocent members of the public. The customers aren't happy with the service.

I have watched policing change over the years. I don't say this lightly or without a significant measure of responsibility and ownership for that change. I don't want it to be where it is now. But I have been a police trainer since the mid-90's, so I am part of the group of trainers who help police officers prepare for the rigors and challenges of policing.

I bear responsibility for the training that has spawned and perpetuated the mindset and training that now presents itself in what is a dysfunctional method of policing. I am talking about fear-based police training.

This method of preparation and training civilian police officers is wreaking havoc on the law enforcement/public relationships in many of our communities.

Though I don't subscribe to, nor teach, fear-based methodology, I accept responsibility for being a member of the cadre that presents the training that has spawned and perpetuated the mindset and poor performance that now presents itself through a dysfunctional and dangerous method of policing.

Law enforcement has become less responsive to the public we protect. We have created and encouraged an 'us versus them" attitude. We see it in how many officers post social media messages about "the problem" being the public, not police.

This disconnect is seen in the sarcasm from LE about the current move to legalize and decriminalize many types of narcotics, as though the public is clueless and ignorant if they believe drugs should be legal and available.

I see and hear officers around the country complain about how the public doesn't appreciate their sacrifice, the value of their lives, and even worse, their requirement to work holidays.

I listen to these laments and then consider this. In the four months it took me to write this book, the following happened:

1) Police shot and killed Bennie Edwards, a homeless man with significant mental health issues (paranoia, schizophrenia), when he wouldn't drop a knife as officers converged on him in a strip mall parking lot.

2) A police officer shot and killed Andre Hill as Hill walked toward him holding only a cell phone.

3) A Texas police officer shot and killed 52-year-old pastor Patrick Warren Sr., after tasing him. The pastor was unarmed, and the original call was a mental health assist request made by the pastor's family.

4) Sheriff deputies in California shot and killed Betty Francois, a 91-year-old homeowner after they say she pointed a shotgun in their direction and wouldn't comply with their commands, when they responded to *her* 911 call about an intruder in *her* home. **Betty was legally blind and deaf**.

5) Revelations have now come out that a Louisville, KY PD detective lied about probable cause in obtaining the no-knock warrant that resulted in Breonna Taylor's killing in March of 2020.

6) It has been determined that dozens of law enforcement officers (30+ as of January 25, 2021), participated in, or aided the mob that rioted and attacked the US Capitol on January 6, 2021, in an apparent effort to delay the ratification of the 2020 Presidential election. In other words, former and current police officers were part of an attempted coup of the United State of America's electoral process.

7) Police on a mental health call in Rochester, NY pepper sprayed and handcuffed a 9-year-old because she wouldn't put her feet into a police car. We could have stopped at handcuffed a 9-year-old.

8) Just added. (Seriously, you can't make this up) In February, just outside Denver, Colorado, police officers shot and killed a middle-aged woman because they had been told "a party" involved in a police call had a gun. The lady they shot and killed was unarmed. The details are still under investigation.

Now these are the big stories. There are the almost daily video postings of police verbally berating a citizen, threatening to abuse constitutional rights, or outright lying to people. All these events taking place, and some law enforcement officers still want to say the public is the problem. Technically, I agree with them.

> "The police are the public,
> the public are the police."
>
> -Sir Robert Peel [1]

If law enforcement is to regain public image and trust or at least improve from where we are now, we must see the issues that WE, law enforcement, have created. Policing cannot continue to sit in a 360-degree protection fire base and point its finger at the public and say, "The public is the problem."

Going the Wrong Direction

Law enforcement has circled the wagons. We put out social media posts that say, "The police don't need to be retrained, the public needs to be retrained." We cite debunked studies [2] that claim police don't shoot more Black people than white people. We seem ready to spout statistics until the last police department gets defunded and shuts down, because "facts don't care about your feelings."

I have listened as officers called protesters animals for burning police cars and breaking store windows, then dismissed the malfeasance of Breonna Taylor's killing by narcotics detectives who, now it appears, were in her house illegally, and violated all known law enforcement firearms training by shooting without identifying their threat/target and beyond.

There was a whole social media smear campaign against Taylor, painting her as involved in drugs and incorrectly saying her boyfriend was a drug dealer. This information was all false, as a quick internet check can confirm. Taylor wasn't involved in drugs, but the detectives engaged in felony perjury.

Time for Introspection

We are at a crossroads. 2020 was a big year of extremely questionable police shootings and killings of citizens. We can choose to continue the way we have been, as I have outlined above. We can do the same and get the same results. Or we can do something different. We can listen.

If we look past the rhetoric, we may see some truth. We in policing are failing our public. We are not providing the same great service to all of our citizens.

Yes, some police officers do an amazing job. Many are satisfactory and most others do not mess up too much. But I will never agree with the inaccurate rhetoric that "99.9% of police are doing a great job [3]."

I have been in policing since 1992. I have taught all over the country and outside the United States. I will agree that a tiny minority of officers wreak havoc on communities, committing crimes and otherwise abusing their authority. Way fewer than one in ten. A little negativity goes a long way.

It is said a DUI driver will drive drunk or impaired 80 times before being caught their first time. As with DUI drivers, we only see the visible part of the iceberg when it comes to police abuses. We see the big mess-ups.

Police officers acting officiously, behaving badly, using excessive and inappropriate force is nothing new. We just see it more now because of smartphones and social media.

Public viewing of police interactions really began when Rodney King was videotaped being beaten by LAPD officers, and the officers gave a different account of the event than was recorded by a bystander and witnessed by the world.

Broad based, intrinsic societal inequities definitely contributed to those officers not being held accountable for excessively beating a noncombative person and lying about it afterwards.

Since then, the recording of police interactions has become standard operating procedure by both law enforcement and the general public. We have even seen police officers kill people on a live internet video stream.

Philando Castile was shot 7 times while performing an officer-directed task [4]. He was told to retrieve his driver's license by the very officer who shot him.

You can try to argue, but Castile never presented a threat to Geronimo Yanez. Not even up to the moment Yanez shot him 7 times, as Castile's daughter sat directly behind him in a small car.

The "threat" was created by Yanez, in his own mind, from his fear-based training and "I go home" mindset.

Is Racism the Issue?

We hear an increasing call from many in the public that these incidents are all because of racism, bias, and an almost organizational effort to exterminate minorities. Specifically, Black people.

Bias plays a part in all interactions we have, in and out of policing. Racism, bigotry, and other social or caste-based insecurities enter into the interactions between police and the public at some level much of the time. As a 20-year diversity and cross-cultural communication facilitator, I readily acknowledge that our biases impact all interactions with other people. I also believe that sword cuts both ways.

The public has preconceptions and biases against police that they willingly and enthusiastically maintain and pass on to their family and friends. I have been negatively prejudged for being associated with law enforcement. I spent 20 years connecting with my community in unique and positive ways and still I had strangers call me derogatory names simply because of my chosen profession.

An arrestee once told me the only reason I was taking him to jail was because he was white. He told me if he had been black, I would have gone easier on him.

Race, bias, and hierarchy may be underlying components in interactions gone bad, but they are not overarching factors. There is something different guiding the actions, and inactions, than some hidden desire white police officers have harbored for years to exterminate a group of people.

There is no mass conspiracy to get rid of Black people, or any other minority.

The deficiencies that cause the tragic events we seem to see more of all the time go beyond what can be classified simply as racism or bigotry. How do we account for minority officers who have shot and killed multiple minority members under questionable circumstances? Or white officers who abuse white citizens?

If you believe the answer is simply that all white people (and police officers) "stop being racist" we will never solve the law enforcement problem of using inappropriate or excessive force. Racism is an issue, it's not the issue. As a 25+ year police trainer, I see something else.

Fear, supremacy, power, and other destructive traits are blending together in the panicked overreactions we see too much of in the times of "highly trained professionals." Fear-based belief systems, manifested through fear-based police training, are the most significant components of our overall issues.

Many incidents of police shooting people, especially completely innocent people, would have been avoided if very basic, time-tested and proven principles, concepts, and tactics had been known, taught, and applied. Rather than overt racism, in most cases, I see poor training and decision making. There is an overall failure in police mindset, preparation, and training.

So much heartache can be avoided, so much liability will be reduced, if we change the way we prepare and train our police officers. I train LEOs to be better, more confident, and to be more mindful of their roles and responsibilities. I don't want to see them charged with crimes and imprisoned.

I train Guardians.

In this book, I will discuss what law enforcement is doing to dismantle and damage public trust and image. I will talk about the ways we create the bad situation, the tragedies, and how we can change our perceptions to improve our performance.

This book is about where we are, where we want to go, and how we can get there.

But unlike most books about police reform, the answer doesn't lie on the other side of multiple blue-ribbon commissions, spending thousands of dollars and months of time to determine that a growing segment of the population doesn't trust or respect the police.

Street officers know this dynamic all too well. By the time a commission is needed to "see if there is a problem", everyone already knows there is a problem.

They see it in NYC when people dump buckets of water (I hope it was water) on police officers' heads as they are simply doing their jobs. Street officers feel the lack of respect as they get taunted by crowds that gather as they just try to work a crime scene in Detroit, where other officers just shot a man who chased them with a knife.

LEOs know there is a problem when they are ambushed and shot in the face by a criminal as they simply sit in their marked patrol vehicle in Los Angeles.

We are beyond asking is there a problem. We know there is. And while the public plays a role, contrary to a social media post attributed to former Wisconsin Sheriff David Clarke [5], between the public and police the only group who has been trained are the police.

The police are the ones who need to be retrained.

But it isn't a bad thing. We have had too much on our plates. Like a child at a buffet, our parent overloaded our plate with too much good food.

Now we sit at the table, not realizing we could take our time. And we don't need to eat all the food. We didn't take it. It was picked for us. All we wanted was Jello and mac and cheese any way.

The law enforcement profession has taken on too many other professions' responsibilities. We are expected to be psychologists, EMTs, child, job, and marriage counselors. Police officers are given a few hours of training in areas requiring advanced degrees and expected to be fully competent. We have become more trained, not better trained.

Our police have become underprepared and overwhelmed.

A Broader Perspective

In police training, we talk about the danger of tunnel vision because one doesn't see everything in front of them, only a tiny portion. We always remind SWAT operators moving in search mode to "stay off their sights", because looking at the world through their sights gives them tunnel vision.

When officers are looking through their sights, they will see the suspect, or whoever is in front of them, from maybe the torso up. But they will not see the person's hands. The hands that will either be empty, showing no threat, or holding a weapon.

If we can't see the whole picture, including the potential for threat, we cannot process critical information accurately and timely.

Taking a broader view of the world, policing, and the public, allows us to "see the hands." People will see a more complete, accurate, and realistic picture of law enforcement. We will see the police officers working diligently in their communities, as the sheepdogs protecting the flock. We will see all the really good things LEOs do to support their communities.

We will also see the abuses. We will see and acknowledge the preventable tragedy of innocent homeowners shot in their own residence. We will see the officers who verbally and physically abuse the public, wreaking havoc on communities by degrading trust, confidence, and relationships.

By removing our emotion, we will be able to see that we actually all want the same thing, effective public safety and comprehensive community satisfaction.

The Real Root of the Problem

I viewed these tragic and negative events as a trainer in a training environment. I looked at the dynamics from the perspective of a trainee and how they may or may not understand my teachings.

I evaluated events and statements of involved officers and if their actions appeared to be consistent with what I teach as a tactics trainer.

I compared the real results with the expected results when using principles and concepts I teach in my police tactics courses. I noticed a disturbing pattern.

Officers involved in questionable shootings, uses of force, or negative interactions, behaved in common ways. In questionable events, officers and agencies gave very rhetorical, superficial explanations of police actions, after the fact.

Depictions and justifications were vague, not specific to the event. They were boilerplate without specificity pertaining to the event. Or the story changed once video was produced, and statements were walked back.

Force options were limited, not correctly utilized, or not fully understood. Tasers were used but were either "ineffective" or didn't work.

These terms are vague in that a Taser may have incapacitated a person for the allotted 5 seconds but didn't afford officers the opportunity to get the person into custody. Or the Taser failed to perform at all due to some variable that prohibited its correct application.

(I believe some officers don't understand the temporary incapacitation concept of Taser. They believe it will render the person semi-conscious for an extended time, like in the movies)

There was usually no coordination and no organization. Nobody appeared to be in charge. Or rather, nobody on the law enforcement side seemed in control of the situation. Sometimes there was a supervisor on scene, but they did nothing to add to the police command and control.

All critical incidents are chaotic. Police are called because a situation has degraded beyond the capabilities of anyone present to handle.

Police restore order from chaos.

If we are only going to show up as helpless and resource deficient as the general public, what good are we?

Based on my understanding of police tactics and critical incident decision-making, from experience, learning, and teaching, I saw these glaring deficiencies in critical incidents as consistent with being woefully unprepared to accomplish a mission or job task.

I believe the key issues most negatively affecting the ability of police officers to fully function as the community guardians people need them to be are:

1) **Preparation**
2) **Training**
3) **Support**

To improve police performance and restore public trust, these three main areas must be addressed and reimagined.

Preparation

We must start by redefining the police officer's role in society as a community guardian rather than as an enemy combatant. LEOs have been told they are at war. At war with drugs, at war with terrorism. At war with the public.

Since 2003, We have been at actual war, with many of our current LEOs having served in the military. They have been to war. They know what the word "war" means. It means to annihilate, eliminate, and bring the enemy into submission.

In war there are two sides, mine and the enemy. Anyone who doesn't look, think, or act like me is the enemy. This is ingrained in soldiers for good reason. It is life preserving and mission accomplishing.

Here at home in our civilian communities saying "we are at war" can lead to confusion and undesired action, to put it mildly.

Police officers–the sheepdogs–are guardians not warriors. Their role is to protect the flock. They must be part of the flock. They also must guard against identifying more with the wolf than with the sheep. Our sheepdog, sheep, wolf analogy needs some updating.

And they must accept that the people they work for and protect will not always look, think, or act like them. But the public is still worthy of service and everyone has life value as human beings.

Though we talk a good game about sacrifice and giving our life in service, too many officers are trained to have a total self-preservation mindset. This runs counter to what effort may be required of them in certain situations.

The "I go home" mindset can create conflict in a critical moment, causing an officer to overreact, under respond, fail to act, or simply not show up. This mindset is how 4 deputies were able stand outside Marjorie Stoneham Douglas High School in Parkland, Florida as almost 20 children and adults were slaughtered inside.

This mindset is how a New York City police officer can, within 2 minutes of arrival, tase, then shoot and kill a man standing in his own kitchen, holding a bread knife and a stick, when the officer showed up simply to evaluate the man's mental health state [6]

Training

We should train our officers in human-centered, principle-based tactics and decision making, that put a strong emphasis on "Why" we use certain tactics in certain situations.

Confidence-building training must replace fear-based training.

Rather than projecting the boogey-man onto the entire community, we should work to grow each officer's competency in self-awareness, self-knowledge, and self-understanding.

Fear breeds panicked reaction. Confidence creates reasoned response.

As trainers, we should teach officers how to think critically, not merely "action regurgitation". The real world has too many variables to cover everything in training. Consider the university approach.

Teach officers how to learn, not just what to know.

This change will grow confidence and improve performance, while also increasing safety for officers and the public. It will also produce officers who are more well-rounded and diverse of thought. Confidence enables police officers to focus on service, not exclusively their own survival.

Police training must address the requirements, parameters, objectives, and goals of civilian law enforcement. We work within the legal parameters of the US Constitution, federal, state, and local laws.

Our tactics must conform to performance requirements such as "no misses are acceptable", justifiable use of force, criminal versus noncriminal contacts, and other considerations soldiers in war don't have.

As a profession, law enforcement should stop thinking that Navy SEAL training will better prepare our police officers to "do battle". Civilian police aren't special forces soldiers.

Teaching our police officers military Close Quarters Battle tactics and then expecting them to do the job like a police officer is like teaching a mechanic to work on cars, then telling them to go build a rocket. Would you want to fly in that rocket?

Military CQB training teaches some really excellent military tactics. But it doesn't teach police tactics. It doesn't teach the "why" of tactics, that is necessary for police to know and understand.
LEOs must be able to explain the reasons for their actions. The most important place an officer will ever explain their work is in a court of law. If we want people to understand what we do, we need to be able to explain what we do, and more important, why we did it.

Support

Organizationally and societally, we must build in the support to help officers develop resilience, emotional strength, and maturity among other qualities. People will do phenomenal things when they feel supported. Police officers will put themselves on the line when they feel they have a "lifeline" attached.

When LEOs don't feel supported, the weight of their responsibility can become too much for a single human being to hold.

We have seen several highly publicized police suicides recently. Two officers who were involved in stopping the attack on the Capitol, and a Black officer in Louisiana who was driven to suicide by the inhumanity, bigotry, and disregard of the public toward police, as well as LEOs toward each other. Police suicides far exceeded police being killed in 2020[7].

Suicides have passed all manners of Line of Duty Deaths (LODD). This is a real indicator that officers don't feel they have backing for when the pressures get too much. Police officers are human beings, not superheroes.
Everything I will talk about as far change can be done at the individual officer level, the shift level, the agency level. The information I present is how most truly effective change happens. From the ground up.

What I do know is that there needs to be change in policing. The public's opinion has validity, and their complaint has merit. Yes, the public also needs to change, but we can't even get people to stop at stop signs. Control of others isn't really a "thing".

WE, the police, need to change. WE are the trained professionals. Since we can't control other people's beliefs, intents, or behaviors, we should simply model by example.

Don't do as I heard a parent say many years ago. "I teach my kid to not respect anyone until they respect my kid."

All I could think is, that's not how any of this works. Well, let's get to it. Let's find out how this does work.

This van operated for over 8 years as a way of connecting to various segments of the public. It was well received and appreciated.

1: The Growing Disconnect

"Houston, We Have a Problem!"

Sometimes people think "pro police" means "never critique". To paraphrase what American author James Baldwin once said about his critique of the USA, "It is precisely because I love policing that I will continue to critique it."

I am 100% pro police.

We can continue to do what we have been doing, defensive posturing, recitation of facts, data, and figures (Facts don't care about your feelings, right?!), and categorically dismissing the critical public as ignorant, unappreciative, and whatever other derogatory term you care to call them. We can do all that, and you know what I do know for sure?

You won't win friends or influence people. Nor will we improve the situation and restore public trust.

More Trained does not Equal Well Trained

I watched an interview by a conservative news outlet anchor with a panel of law enforcement officers, retired and current. There was a police chief, a retired detective, and a representative of a major police union. I personally know the union rep.

This was during the time shortly after the Breonna Taylor shooting, the George Floyd death, and a couple of other incidents. Maybe before the Jacob Blake shooting in Kenosha, WI. Anyway, you get the picture.

There were several use of force incidents that gained national attention, where citizens died at the hands of police and the nationwide protests were in full swing.

The show host was asking about policing and these three panelists are giving superficial and really meaningless answers. By this, I mean they are regurgitating rhetoric that is not doing anything help anyone believe law enforcement even cares about anything other than saving face as a profession.

But it sounded comforting and positive to policing. And confusing to the public, in light of actual events. The host then asked the union rep about police training, and whether police are well trained.

Now, I train police. I also talk to trainers and talk to police. We all know police are not trained well enough. We can never be trained "well enough". We could always be better trained, more trained, etc. But what does he say?

"We are the best trained we have ever been!"

My jaw dropped.

I have much love and respect for this man. He is a fantastic police officer and person and has national credibility in and out of law enforcement.

On national television, in front of an overwhelmingly supportive audience, amid national protests, riots, officers shooting unarmed people, the wrong person, kneeling on peoples' necks until they died, officers hitting people in the face with kinetic baton rounds (not proper application based on threat and training), officers being shot and killed by right wing domestic terrorists, ambushed in their vehicles by gang members, and being assaulted by rioters, he essentially says, "It's all good."

Now you may absolutely agree with him. And that is fine. You would be wrong. And I say that with complete love for the profession, and love for you as a law enforcement professional. Sometimes Always, we need to look at ourselves with a critical eye and accept that a critique the public is giving us might have merit.

"Riot is the language of the unheard."
-Martin Luther King, Jr.

> **Disclaimer:** I do not condone riots as an effective means to encourage public discourse and conciliation. They are too divisive and don't encourage cooperation. But, if they happen, I will take it as a sign that someone has a problem, and I will address the validity of their complaint before I dismiss them and reject their grievance. It may prevent future riots.

What I will also do is lay out everything on the table, take a good look at it, understand what we can use and only after careful inspection and consideration, discard what doesn't make sense. What we keep will benefit policing and the community.

To do this, we must get uncomfortable. We must be ok with being uncomfortable, something that is difficult for law enforcement officers.

Law enforcement must look at itself with the introspective critical eye and possess the willingness to judge itself with the same enthusiasm it judges the general public.

What "Best Trained" Looks Like

We talk about how well trained our US police officers are today, but we don't look at what really constitutes this training. We have given our officers more tasks than ever before.

LEOs are supposed to be everything to everyone, and the public expects 100% effectiveness. 4 hours of training is supposed to make them qualified to act as psychologists, EMTs, and all manner of social workers.

In the effort to give this varied training, LEOs get less tactical decision-making training. We get less shoot/don't shoot firearms training.

I know of police agencies in this country who have one firearms qualification per year. One day in 365 they evaluate their officers' abilities to accurately and successfully deploy their highest liability tool in a critical incident. Let's break that down.

Say an officer in an agency barely qualifies in one year and because they don't shoot "for real" for another year, they don't invest themselves in training during the year. 11 months down the road, what do you think their firearms skills will look like?
Agencies should qualify and train, at least quarterly, since firearms decision-making and practical application (shooting) are perishable skills.

In a recent incident in Oklahoma City, a homeless man with mental health issues (sound familiar?), named Bennie Edwards [8], was in the parking lot of a small strip mall holding a knife. Officers responded and commanded Edwards to drop his knife.

Remember, he is paranoid, and three police officers are closing in, moving toward him, confining him, while yelling and pointing weapons at him. No, Edwards didn't drop the knife.

A taser was deployed. It was not effective.

Watching the video, it is pretty evident why it wasn't effective. Edwards was wearing a heavy canvas-type work coat. And he was moving around. Not ideal conditions, and that's without any other variables that come into play in the real world.

They also attempted to use pepper spray to subdue Mr. Edwards. It wasn't effective. No chemical agent works on everyone all the time or the same way.

So, the officers shot him. That was effective. He died.

Now, regardless of the nature of his offense, criminal or just a crazy man holding a knife, the officers were limited in their response by their tools, tactics, and training.

They didn't have good team tactics. They were three single officers who just happened to be at the same scene.

They didn't use space and time to help in thought processing, and to provide a physical and psychological barrier for the suspect.

Even though Edwards never directly threatened any officer, they perceived his running in their general direction as a focused attack, leading to their use of lethal force.

A plus in this situation is that the officers did try to use less lethal means to subdue Mr. Edwards. Too often, officers don't even try to use intermediate force prior to lethal force. If you can't get past the whole "crazy guy with a knife", here's another one.

A small-town Texas high school athletics coach, Jonathan Price, local-boy-done-good, all around nice guy, witnessed a domestic disturbance at a gas station in Texas [9]. He stopped the assault.

When the police officer showed up, he targeted the coach as the problem. Price walked away from the officer, who, possibly perceiving a dismissal of his authority, tased the coach. Of course, in keeping with the theme, it did not incapacitate Price, and the coach turned toward the officer, possibly incredulous that he has become the recipient of this shocking use of force.

This officer, with 6 months in policing and working at an agency in a town of about 6,000 people (the type of place that has yearly qualifications, a couple hours of formal training in everything else, but its officers are "the best trained we've ever been!") perceived this action as a deadly threat and pulling his gun, shot and killed Price.

Not insignificant to the overall "optics", Price was a Black man. Do you also see where and how people might get a feeling that race plays into these events? Possibly?
Even though the officer in the last case has been charged with a felony, what is the typical response to these types of situations? Yes, you got it. Those boilerplate statements issued by chiefs, sheriffs, and union presidents the country over.
"Police must make split second decisions in a rapidly changing environment."

Or the other get-out-of-jail-free card, "I was in fear for my life."

My question is this. Why do we, as the "best-trained-we've-ever-been" professionals, get to claim to be so scared as to shoot unarmed or non-threatening people, or get to claim situation overwhelm, but the alcohol, drug, or psychosis impaired public doesn't?

Why must the clueless, untrained "sheep", the public, be more coherent, make better "split-second decisions", process information faster, and remain more "cool, calm, and collected" than the trained professionals, who get to react almost blindly out of panic and fear?

In the Atatiana Jefferson tragedy [10], Fort Worth Police Officer Kevin Dean, allowed less than 2 seconds between his command for Ms. Jefferson to show her hands and his shot that killed her. He didn't even allow Ms. Jefferson time to process the situation according to the OODA Loop information processing paradigm.

She would have needed time to Observe his presence and then his command, Orient herself to what he was commanding, Decide her course of action, then Act.

We will discuss how this critical paradigm is often disregarded and misunderstood by police yet plays a foundational role in actions taken by all people in everything we do.
How long do you think it might take her, as an untrained civilian, to orient herself to the reality of the situation, at 2am, standing in her house, holding a gun because she may have perceived the officer as an intruder?

How long for her to go from "There's an intruder lurking outside my window" to "Oh, that's no intruder, it is a police officer lurking outside my window"?

Obviously longer than the two seconds Dean was willing to give her. How about the Breonna Taylor shooting?

Some people said, well her fiancé Kenneth Walker shot first, so the detectives were well within their rights to shoot back. Let's break it down.

1) The warrant was served at midnight. What are most regular, normal people doing at midnight? Normal, not police. Yes, sleeping.

2) Taylor had, at one time in the past, been involved with a drug dealer. But Kenneth Walker, her fiancé, was not, nor is one. And he is a registered firearm owner.

3) The officers, though they changed their story several times during the subsequent investigation, had a no-knock warrant exception, and did not wait a significant time between breaching the door and making entry. Only one witness, out of many, corroborated detectives' claims they identified themselves as law enforcement prior to making entry. Walker called 911 to report a break in, not realizing the intruders were police.

4) Walker said that Taylor's ex-boyfriend, the actual drug dealer and focus of the case, had threatened him in the past.

Walker and Taylor were awakened by the breach of their front door. Walker legitimately and legally armed himself. This is a resident's worst-case scenario. Someone breaking into their house in the middle of the night.

As the couple exited the bedroom, they saw large, silhouetted figures (detectives wearing body armor) standing in their front doorway yelling.

Walker fired one round, low, striking a detective in the leg. One round, intended to, at worst, wound. Does that sound like someone who is trying to take on the police? Of course not.

My opinion: This case is horrible, because of the terrible tactical decision making of these narcotics detectives. Their actions, and the smear campaign against Ms. Taylor is an example of the depth of the problem in policing that we refuse to acknowledge.

These examples are to point out how we give the trained professional law enforcement officers the excuse of being in fear for their lives, or that they need to make split second decisions to prevent their injury or death, but we don't give that same allowance to the untrained, panicked public.

I truly hope this is making sense to readers who may not have thought about things this way before. I really do. If you don't get it, I ask you to keep working to understand it.

If you are in policing and feel your life is so much more important than anyone else's, that when you handle a call to help a suicidal or mental health compromised person, all you can worry about is keeping yourself safe above all others, my suggestion is don't go.

You will be no help to anyone.

Overriding fear for your own safety will prevent you making good decisions that benefit anyone else.

Forgive easily,
Learn quickly,
Act inentionally

2: How We Learn

"My lens colors my world"

Without this becoming a tutorial on education, I will give this brief illustration of two ways we can intake information and use it to form our knowledge. We can assimilate information, or we can accommodate the information.

Accommodation and Assimilation

I will explain the difference between the two, using an analogy from the book, *Nonsense, The Power of Not Knowing* [11], by Jamie Holmes.

When we assimilate information, we take in new information, and process it by judging it against what we already know or believe to be true. Picture seeing a white crow for the first time. You only know crows to be black, but here stands a white one.

If you assimilate this new information, you will determine that since you have never known crows to be white this cannot be a crow and must be some

other white bird. It's a crow, but your need for certainty and order won't let you accept this new information.

Your conviction in your held beliefs prevents you from accepting this new information. It cannot be true. This new information cannot occupy the space reserved for the color of crows.

When we accommodate information, we create more space and allow for the possibility that there is new information we have not previously known. Now when you see a white crow, you simply say, "Wow! A white crow. I have never seen that before."

No internal argument. No worry about this uncertainty in your world. To carry it further, if crows can be black and now white, what other colors might they be?

You have none of that confliction associated with new information that challenges your already held beliefs. You are excited to see all the colors crows might come in.

Police officers, because of our traits, strong sense of value, and character, are generally assimilators. We don't like uncertainty. We don't like ambiguity.

We want to know that the person's hands are empty. We need to know they have no weapons in their pockets. We must find out what that person is "up to" standing in the shadows over there.

LEOs have a difficult time just allowing things to develop. We like to "help" things develop. Even compel them to develop. We don't like to just sit back and observe. Except narcs. Narcs will sit and observe all day.

If we can be comfortable with uncertainty, we might see our world in a different way. We don't need to immediately fit people into the categories of "friend" or "foe".

We might work to be ok with presuming the person has a weapon, but as long as they don't reach in their pocket and pull it out, they will stay alive. I understand. It feels like uncertainty can be deadly.

Being uncomfortable with uncertainty increases danger, not uncertainty itself.

We will work on being uncomfortable with uncertainty. Right now, we are just learning how we learn.

If we aren't aware of how we process information, and the pros and cons to our methods, we will never learn as much as we need, or as well as we should.

Perception versus Intent

This is my own theory. I came by this theory watching many incidents, and through thousands of hours training police.

This dynamic is important to understanding how we process information presented to us since it causes us to have a preconceived idea of what the other person is planning to do. It causes us to "pre guess" the thoughts of a total stranger.

Alfredo Saldivar

In September 2020, a Prescott Valley AZ PD k9 bit Alfredo Saldivar after a car chase. Saldivar, out of the car, was kneeling with his hands raised as instructed. He pulled his shirt up to show he had no weapons. He was cooperative with the officers' commands.

One officer told him to stand. As he stood up, the K9 handler perceived Saldivar was not being compliant. either he didn't hear the command, or he just processed the information different. Whichever, the K9 was released. It bit Saldivar, causing significant injury.

Here is a case where perception and intent collided. Saldivar intended to comply. He had followed commands since he got out of his vehicle. He stood up at the command one of the officers.

The handler perceived something very different than the commands officer perceived. One perceived Saldivar as being cooperative enough to take into custody in a standing position. The other did not. Saldivar never intended to disobey the police at that point.

Perception is what *we* interpret or determine a situation or condition to be.

This interpretation is based on our knowledge, experience, belief system, and other building blocks in our total personality makeup. Perception is like wearing a certain shade of glasses.

Our perception colors the world we see. Some see yellow, some see purple. Even when two people see the same basic color, the shade will be different because everyone has a unique perspective of the world and subsequently, their perception of it.

Intent is *how* we plan to act, or *why* we mean to do something.

Two people may have the same action or similar behavior, but for completely different reasons.

I may push you down to hurt you, or I may push you down to push you out of the path of an object hurtling at you. The action is the same, but the intent is different. One is to hurt you, the other to keep you from being hurt.

We incorrectly train our police that a weapon in hand is a weapon in play. We correctly train our police that anything can be used as a weapon. A person holding a gun may not be intent on committing a crime with it, but we should perceive anything can be a potential weapon.

Anything, including the most seemingly innocent child's toy, can be used to hurt or kill, if used in certain ways. A bowl of soup can nourish a person or be used to drown them. Would you perceive a bowl of soup as food, or as a weapon? Do you intend to feed someone, or kill them?

One person's intent can be misread because of another person's perception. This misinterpretation, or misperception of intent, has led to many tragedies in police contacts with citizens.

When I worked patrol and responded to domestic disturbances, I chuckled when our dispatchers would tell us there were "no weapons in the house".

I pictured a completely empty house, no furniture, no cooking utensils, pots or pans, nothing. Sterile. I viewed two armless, legless people sitting in the middle of an empty living room, just waiting for me to walk in. I knew what the resident/caller and our dispatcher were thinking.

No swords, guns, bazookas, tanks, and short-range bombers.

Police officers see everything as a potential weapon, because people have used close to every substance imaginable, manmade or existing in nature, to harm others. LEOs know you can kill with soup. More than one way.

So, as officers enter a situation, they focus on their perception of what a person is able to do with an object, more than what the person intends to do with the object. This is where the problem starts.

Police officers are drilled about personal safety, the danger of everything, and the cruelty of humans toward each other. Working in these very negative paradigms is how police officers develop and "justify" their fear of others.

A major consideration in many of these types of incidents, especially when dealing with mental health breaks, is to remember the person may have possessed the "weapon" prior to officer arrival. This would indicate the person did not intend to use the item as a weapon against the police.

It is more reasonable and probable to believe, at most, the person considered the item as a defensive weapon for their own safety, rather than an offensive weapon to be used against law enforcement.

Police officers must understand the correlation between perception and intent. We must also understand the disconnect between them. The majority of use-of-force training for police doesn't account for, and actually discourages, the consideration of these dynamics.

The argument is that situations evolve too quickly for the officer to have time to consider the suspect/subject's intent. The belief is it is better for the officer to err on the side of caution and just use the level of force they feel will best protect them.

Unfortunately, this has led to unarmed, nonthreatening, even innocent people being killed by police. And these tragedies have contributed to the overall feeling that police no longer serve in the best interest of the public, and the loss of public trust now permeating many communities.

Law enforcement must work harder in the training environment to develop the critical thinking skills and confidence in officers to allow their perception and decision-making processing to accommodate for and consider intent.

I am not suggesting LEOs develop these skills in real situations. Real life is where we evaluate the effectiveness of our skills, training is where we develop them. This increased training effort will help to regain public trust and repair relationships.

The OODA Loop

Most of us in policing and the military are familiar with the OODA Loop processing theory as developed many years ago by Air Force pilot Col. John Boyd. I recommend you read some of the books written about him, and the OODA Loop, if you want to dive really deep into this theory.

This theory is everything to understanding how human beings process information in any instance where we do anything. It is so important to understand this for interpersonal interaction and communication in our world.

What I have learned over the years is that, while officers may have heard of it or even learned about it, not many truly understand the depth of the significance of this processing to how we do our jobs, and how the public reacts to us when we do our jobs.

I believe if we all had a better understanding how this process guides our every decision and action, many of the tragedies, officer shootings, even just uses of force, would be greatly mitigated. Here is a brief overview because it is so instrumental in understanding how people think and process information in order to take action.

The OODA Loop theory of information processing operates like this:

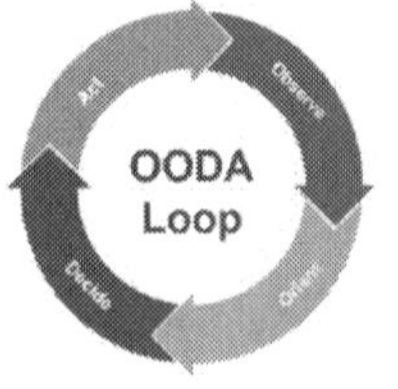

Observe Orient Decide Act

To do anything, a person must go through these four phases. I must observe or recognize a task to be done or considered. I must orient myself to it. Is it something important? Do I need to do anything about it? I then decide what will be my course of action, if any. Last, I act.

From changing careers to brushing your teeth, everything we do flows like this. Big problems arise when we skip or omit a step, or we don't understand the importance of passing through all the steps, in order.

Using our toothbrushing example, consider if you skipped any step. Don't observe your morning breath, you never brush your teeth. Don't brush your teeth, everyone else observes your morning breath. Any step omitted leads to an unsatisfactory outcome.

This theory is so important to law enforcement because, in any situation, it tells us what to do and how to do it. It gives us a blueprint that we can use to prepare ourselves to act.

Knowing we must take these steps helps us better understand the basic premise of police training. And no, it's not so you go home. That is a benefit. The primary function of police training is to decrease our OODA loop processing time. I will say it again:

> **The primary function of police training is to decrease our OODA Loop processing time.**

The flip side to this coin is the other person involved in the situation; the suspect or subject. They go through the OODA loop too. It's not just for us. This is where I see many police officers make mistakes.

Officers fail to account for the need for the other person to work through their own OODA loop, at their own pace of ability, in order to comply with police commands.

Or officers set themselves as the standard or norm for speed and competency in moving through the processing loop. Both lead to catastrophes.

Dylan Ray Scott

A low level wanted fugitive, was spotted by Florida sheriff's deputies. While trying to contact him, Dylan Scott drove a short distance and crashed his SUV into another car. Deputies removed all other people to safety and began trying to talk Scott into surrender.

Scott initially told the deputy he was armed but would not show his hands. (You know where this is going right?).

After watching a four-minute recording consisting mostly of "show me your hands" which the suspect would not do, and "don't make me shoot you", which the suspect eventually got the deputy to do, I realized some things.

Scott understood the OODA Loop better than the deputy. His goal was to have the deputy shoot him. Scott understood that by proximity, the deputy would need to suddenly react to his actions, not respond. Though the suspect probably never learned the actual process, he understood the pros and cons.

Scott forced the deputy to short cut his processing loop and, based on the totality of the situation, make what I consider to be a poor decision. The suspect was never armed.

You may be thinking, "the deputy didn't know that and had to take the word of the suspect". This is true.

If the deputy truly understood the OODA loop, he would have changed everything with one simple action: moving from the driver's window to behind the vehicle. This is the concept of space and time, and we will cover that later.

By staying close to the suspect, and engaging in action versus reaction, the deputy didn't allow *himself* to properly use his OODA loop in his decision making. And the deputy stayed inside the suspect's OODA Loop.

The suspect had previously talked about committing suicide by cop. Even though the deputy didn't know that claim in that moment, he remained static for 4 minutes in a situation where the suspect wasn't complying with a simple, well-known command. Everyone knows the first thing you do is show a police officer your empty hands with the universal surrender signal, "hands up".
The deputy should have realized his commands were not working, and the best course of action was to do something else.

Taking control of ourselves in such moments can do a very important thing. It can break our tunnel vision and allow us to see a bigger picture. It also allows us to think contingencies. "Something else".

Most suspects have only one plan. They don't do contingencies.

If we stay inside their OODA Loop, we increase their confidence that their plan is working. By staying near the vehicle and just repeating the same phrases over and over, the deputy gave the suspect the impression that the suspect was in control.

The deputy showed he continued to believe the suspect's lie about being armed and would react accordingly when the suspect could properly provoke him.

The other half of police training is this. We use police tools and tactics to increase the suspect's OODA loop processing time. Once again:

> **We use police tools and tactics to increase the suspect's OODA loop processing time.**

Don't get this confused. We want to move faster from observation to action (decrease time), while making the suspect slower to action (increase time).

The other person may process at a different pace than you. We can't presume they are as coherent, lucid, or sober as us. We become lulled by the response of role players and partner officers during training.
In training, the "suspects" (role players) always follow our commands and understand exactly what we want them to do. This is not the way when the suspect is intoxicated, psychotic, disabled, deaf, blind, or doesn't understand the language we are speaking to them.

In training, the "suspects" always follow our commands and understand exactly what we want them to do. This is not the way when the suspect is intoxicated, psychotic, disabled, deaf, blind, or doesn't understand the language we are speaking.

Think about simple field sobriety tests. The drunker the person is, the harder it is for them to process the direction that you want them to "just stand still and watch". They keep fidgeting, trying to balance, start the action prematurely, and talking, until you can't continue the test.

Atatiana Jefferson

When he killed Atatiana Jefferson, Fort Worth, TX police officer Kevin Dean was responding to a report of an open front door in the middle of the night. He was not responding to any sort of criminal call. He was sneaking and peeking around Jefferson's windows, when Dean saw Jefferson standing inside, allegedly holding a gun. I say allegedly because a gun was found near her body.

But remember this was Ms. Jefferson's house, in the middle of the night, and perhaps she had already seen the officer's shadows and perceived him to be someone intent on breaking in.

Don't fall into the trap of thinking everyone must automatically recognize you as the police just because you know you are the police. Even in uniform, I sometimes had trouble convincing some people I was a police officer.
Either intoxication, darkness, or some other obstacle prevented them from recognizing my authority. Don't take it personal, just help them work through it.

Dean saw Ms. Jefferson through the window, yelled, "Show me your hands!" and shot her within 2 seconds. The officer ran through his OODA loop processing, but what didn't he do?

He didn't allow Ms. Jefferson to run through hers. He didn't give her time to process that the criminal she saw sneaking around her house at 2am was really a police officer.

The officer assimilated that anyone holding a gun, other than himself, must be a criminal. Had Dean accommodated the information he received, he would have been open to the reality that Jefferson was standing in her house in the middle of the night and not actively committing a crime, but merely holding a firearm.

Dean perceived that "a gun in hand is a gun in play". This detrimental axiom has led to several shootings of innocent civilians in Alabama, Texas, Oklahoma, Arizona, and other states.

What Dean also didn't take time to consider was Jefferson's intent. His lack of observation led to an incorrect orientation, decision, and action. And a horrible tragedy, including Dean now being prosecuted for a capital offense.

Dean created the criminal episode in his mind based on his perception that anyone holding a weapon must be a criminal or engaged in criminal activity. Dean perceived Jefferson's intent to protect herself as a criminal action and possible threat to someone, most likely him.

Police officers must consider how other people might process information and what factors might prohibit them from immediately understanding and complying with instructions.

We can't dismiss this crucial step by saying we don't have time to consider it. Proper mindset preparation, confidence, and proper training will enable us to take time to consider the other person.

Hopefully this has given you some insight and new understanding about how important it is for us to know how we learn, how we process information, and on what we base our actions.

If we don't understand these concepts, we can't be the problem solvers we claim to be. We will use a lot less force if we learn these lessons. We will kill a lot fewer innocent people.

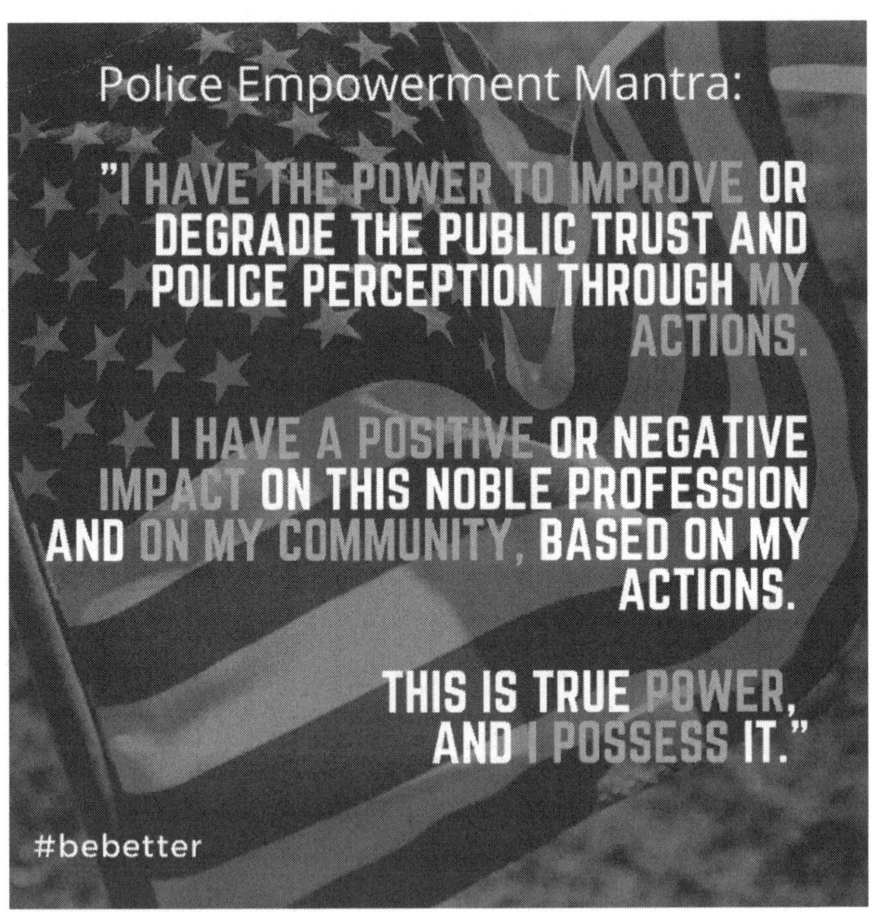
Police Empowerment Mantra:
"I HAVE THE POWER TO IMPROVE OR DEGRADE THE PUBLIC TRUST AND POLICE PERCEPTION THROUGH MY ACTIONS.
I HAVE A POSITIVE OR NEGATIVE IMPACT ON THIS NOBLE PROFESSION AND ON MY COMMUNITY, BASED ON MY ACTIONS.
THIS IS TRUE POWER, AND I POSSESS IT."
#bebetter

My mantra.

3: Race, Bigotry, and Bias

Nothing funny, Bigotry Sucks

Suspend your political ideologies, personal beliefs, etc., and merely allow the possibility to exist that there may be a racial double standard in our country. Now allow that the police are firmly caught up in it, whether or not we realize it.

Racially motivated crimes have increased since 2017 by double-digit percentages, the largest increase in the past decade [12].

Almost daily we see another social media video of someone berating another person based on skin color or ethnicity. Our society has issues. Studies show that policing does not enforce the law equally. I agree with this finding. I am not talking about the intent.

I believe law enforcement officers go out with the intent to be equal, impartial, etc. However, there are unconscious, generationally ingrained influences that prohibit that intent from becoming action.

We each view and move through this world different, based on our experiences and influences. It cannot be helped. Policing's majority population, white males, in general view the public through a certain lens. Especially across cultures. Think about people you know. Think about yourself.

How many of us can honestly say we are able, and willing, to truly look at the world from another person's perspective?

What about if that perspective is very different from our own?

Even if we want to show empathy, compassion, and understanding, it is difficult to do. I do know that not "All White people are racists."

What I also know is that every human being alive has various biases, prejudices, and bigotries that impact how they view, perceive and interact with their world and the people around them.

I believe that it is almost unavoidable for people in the majority population to develop a sense that their view is the normal or standard view. Their perspective somehow holds more credibility and validity than any other views. This is not their fault.

Their perspective and experiences are the ones most often displayed in media, entertainment, politics, etc. The way they see the world is more familiar. Consider the image in your mind when someone says, "Act like an American". What is an "American"? What do we portray as American in our mass media and mass entertainment? What does an "American" look and act like?

If America is a melting pot of cultures and everyone is accepted, how can there be one defined, "acceptable" portrayal of an "American"?

Racial inequality and inequity are woven into the fabric of our collective DNA and surely as the red, white, and blue colors in our nation's flag. This is nothing to be shocked, surprised, or even embarrassed about. It just is. The embarrassment is if we know it exists but do nothing to eradicate it.

Consider how many centuries this bigotry and discrimination has been in the creation, growth, and denial of its negative impact on our country. We have only recently made illegal most forms of systematic discrimination.

We have experienced state sanctioned discrimination within two generations, many of whom were discriminated against are still living. Think about "colored" drinking fountains, "Sundown Towns", or Japanese people forced into concentration camps during World War II.

For centuries, discrimination and bias were legal, written into many states' laws. It is no wonder we have such a hard time acknowledging them as wrong and working to extricate them from our consciousness. For so long, they were legally "right".

The Declaration of Independence proclaims, "all men are created equal" and that all have an "unalienable right to life, liberty, and the pursuit of happiness". It was written by a man who owned enslaved people.

The people of the British colonies in America revolted against what they considered to be oppression, while at the same time, oppressing entire groups of people.

I do believe there is a disparity in policing between races. The disparity is society-wide and has its origin in the centuries old development of our country based on an economically driven racial divide. It also includes the teaching of the superiority of one group over other groups. But that is a deep dive for another time, another book.
Law enforcement must never be beholden or partial to any particular group. It must not even appear partisan or play favorites between our societal groups. I think police unions should definitely not officially endorse any specific political candidate for office. Ever.

Origins of Modern Policing

There is growing rhetoric that US policing is a continuing vestige of our antebellum slavery system.

Speaking for myself, I think Black people are simply trying to understand why long experienced, "familiar" tragedies and lack of improvements seem to continue unchecked, even as many in policing claim, "Everything is fine."

Modern US policing is not based on the southern states antebellum slave patrols. We can more accurately equate the Ku Klux Klan as an extension of slave patrols, even though the KKK was organized during the Reconstruction period [13]. Or even modern bail bond/fugitive recovery agents.

Modern policing is actually modeled after Sir Robert Peel's vision of policing and public safety/law enforcement when he created the London Metropolitan Police in 1829. Peel established a public safety and law enforcement model founded on a professional, accountable police force.

This group of law officers used crime prevention techniques, formal codified laws, and ongoing education in criminal investigation techniques to become an effective and recognized public safety resource.

Today we operate in the spirit of Peel's creation, but in our efforts to be crime fighters we have abandoned a comprehensive desire and effort to be seen as, and view ourselves as, guardians of the public.

Because of our extensive interaction with criminals, and our efforts on behalf of the general public to catch them, we have created a dangerous mindset. We have become like the wolves.

In our effort to hunt criminals, for our own safety, everyone has become a threat. Anyone not a sheepdog is a wolf. We must train and prepare our officers to develop a stronger connection and identification with the flock, the general public.

I am not advocating a lack of officer safety or situational awareness. On the contrary, **human-centered, principle-based training develops a much more confident and competent officer** than fear-based training.

The critical thinking skills, tactics, and decision making I have learned and now teach, have helped thousands of police officers over the last 3 decades solve critical incidents successfully, and in keeping with their oath of office.

4: Data, Facts, and Feelings

"Feelings don't care about your facts"

I get asked all the time in conversations or in interviews, how we got to the place where the public doesn't trust the police. We can say police are a modern version of runaway slave patrols (I disagree), so their very existence is rooted in oppression of minorities.

We can say police are nothing but the servants of the wealthy, kept around to keep the huddled masses at bay. "Jack-booted thugs" of the oppressors...

"All police, 99.9% (right?) are doing a fantastic job–couldn't be better–so anybody who has a problem with US policing is an idiot and knows nothing."

Or that police must "make split second decisions in a rapidly changing environment".

We can even say everyone shot by the police, regardless of whether or not they were justifiable shootings, should have "just listened to the officer."

We can say whatever we want. But the reality of it is that "we are here". We are in this hole and the shovels we used to dig it won't get us out. We need new, different tools. And we need help.

Law enforcement sounds naïve or oblivious, but definitely arrogant when we deny any substantial problem exists. Or when we put the responsibility for a solution on everyone else. 2020 saw several months of sometimes violent protests caused by perceived and actual police abuses and very poor law enforcement decision-making.

If we don't want to acknowledge any problem exists, or this profession needs improvement, the public will take every opportunity to show us just how wrong we are. And they will question and discount every decision you make, even when it is correct and appropriate. We see this when people protest, and question even righteous uses of force.

The Numbers Don't Lie...

I have long wondered how it is that a growing number of people believe US policing appears to be slanted against minorities. Could it be the fact that a Black man is almost 3 times more likely than a white man to be shot by a police officer? This is true. Check the data, I did.

The numbers and statistics I gathered are from the FBI, the National Law Enforcement Officer's Memorial Fund Page, and other pro police sources. I purposely did not gather information from historically anti or even police neutral organizations. I chose police positive sources.

I hear all the time, "Police shoot twice as many White people than they do Black people", as if that's something to be proud of in the first place. Of the 963 people killed by police in 2019, White people accounted for 399 and Black people for 214. Raw numbers only mean something if the populations of both groups are equal.

The numbers aren't equal.

The US white population [14] is around 250M (70+%), while the Black population is around 42M (13%). This puts the Black population at about 1/6th the white population.

Based on raw population numbers, twice as many white people as black people are shot by the police. But the Black population in the US is only 1/6 of the white population.

If we make the population sizes equal, a Black person is around 3 times more likely to be killed by a police officer than a white person.

Yes, this does include suspects in criminal episodes, suspects who attempt to use weapons against police, and any other time police use lethal force against the public. The point to understand is that police use lethal force against Black people at a higher rate than they use it against white people, regardless of the reason. Black people are not 3X more aggressive or assaultive toward police than White people.

The War on Police The facts and data also don't bear out the claim of a "war on cops". I looked into police Line of Duty Deaths (LODDs) and found some interesting information. This is corroborated by and posted on the National Law Enforcement Officers Memorial Website. Here it is. It is actually really good news.

Police LODDs have dropped continuously since 1970. They have declined through every Presidential administration. The most dangerous time in the last century to be a police officer was the 1920's, during prohibition.

During the Obama administration, all line of duty deaths from illnesses to murder, dropped to the lowest they had been in 50 years, on average. During President Trump's administration, LODDs continued to drop, setting new record lows.

The www.nleomf.org website 2020 fatality report lists 48 officers shot and killed in 2020. The report does not break out the other types or murder. But taking the data from the last decade, we can presume, on average, an additional 8 intentional acts that resulted in officer deaths. 2020 saw a **6% decrease in officer murders** compared to 2019.

In 2020, we lost twice as many officers to suicide, and to COVID, each, as we did to murder.

In a televised address in August of 2020, the President of the NYPD New York Police Union Mike O'Meara said that police officers make 350 million contacts each year, on average [15]. This is a huge number!

This number averages to about 500 individual interactions per officer, per year, based on a total law enforcement officer number of around 700K [16].

In a 2000-hour work year, a law enforcement officer is interacting with someone once every 4 hours. We know that not all LEOs have that amount of contact, obviously a patrol officer will interact with more people than say a park ranger, or FBI agent.

Using this number of contacts, O'Meara was illustrating that the incidents of police shooting people, police even using force, is a very low occurrence. And he is correct. But if we apply those numbers to justify the war on police, how do they stack up?

If each law enforcement officer in the United States, some 700,000+, were to make 500 contacts per year, police officers have the following chances of either dying or being killed while on duty.

Police: Chance of dying on duty,
intentional, accidental, or natural=1 in 2M

Chance of being killed on duty=1 in 5M

Reminder: White civilians/subjects/suspects:
Chance of being killed by police=1 in 600k

Black civilians/subjects/suspects:
Chance of being killed by police=1 in 200k

Police are 5-10 times less likely to be killed during police/public interactions than the public.

It puts the claim of a war on police in a much more objective light. But really, why are these numbers important? Shouldn't even one officer's death be too many? To the second question I would simply say yes. To the first, I say the following.

The same numbers can be used by both sides to prove their points. From the perspective of the public, and minorities, the numbers show the police are killing minorities at a disproportionately higher rate. On the police side the numbers show the police aren't killing that many people.

Law enforcement and its supporters use the same numbers to defend the fear-based mindset that police could be attacked at any moment. While the possibility of a line of duty death exists, the data suggests that the average officer will work for 20 years before the statistical odds even begin to put them in danger.
Understand, I am only illustrating that we have succumbed to the belief in an epidemic of violence against police that doesn't exist. And this belief has greatly contributed to the fear-based insecurity that has become the foundation of our police mindset preparation and training.

We are planning for, preparing for, training for, and fighting a war that doesn't exist, but has been created in our minds. And it is both literally and figuratively killing the public trust and relationships.

But the Numbers Don't Cry, Either...

I say we stop using numbers and data to try to prove that police don't kill that many people, and that people are slaughtering police. The numbers don't add up.

The numbers don't lie. But more important, the numbers don't cry.

When we use cold facts, data, and numbers, we can distance ourselves from the human factor, the human loss of the situation. Killing, death, and dying is an event that happens between human beings. We need to keep that dynamic forefront. We may be more responsible with other peoples' lives if we do.

The killing of a person is nothing nice. It is messy, sad, and creates a tragic ripple effect in any community where it happens. How we consider or dismiss the deaths, killings, and murders says a lot about the value we give to the person as a human being.

Everyone who dies or is killed is a human being.

What they did or didn't do to precipitate their death, may or may not be relevant or justify their death or killing. We definitely shouldn't dehumanize the innocent people we kill in the effort to reduce our guilt in killing them.

Attacks on Law Enforcement

A person who attacks a law enforcement officer has gone a long way towards forfeiting their life. Police defensive tactics training is designed to develop an officer's ability to protect themselves and others from various manners of personal attack.

It is not up for discussion, if someone attacks me, I use maximum effort to stop that person from attacking me or anyone else ever again. The person will either learn this lesson and never do it again, or they will die. If they die, the sum total of their existence will be to serve as an example to others.

I believe and train, and always have, that if someone attacks me and they are still conscious when they hit the ground, I didn't do my best job in educating them on their mistake.

Being a police officer means you might have other people purposefully attack you because of the authority you represent or because you are going to deprive them of their freedom.

There is a warped belief in our society that somehow police officers forfeit their lives, and it is almost expected of them to be killed. There is zero percent acceptable casualty rate in policing.

Police officers are not expendable.

Already in 2021 (early February), 8 officers have been killed in the line of duty. This is a 33% increase over this time in 2020. This should not be acceptable to anyone. It may be understandable since LEOs insert themselves into dangerous incidents, but it should never become unremarkable or "to be expected".

We as a society, must shift to acknowledging that each life is a human being, and each loss of life is significant to all of us. If I do not see you as having value, how can I expect you to see the value in me?

5: Expect Less, Require More

"Underprepared, overwhelmed"

Training police in a national and international arena has given me insight into the relationship between community and policing at a level that not many people get to see, learn about, and understand. I am a student of people, and part of my educational journey is to understand and help improve this strained relationship between the public and law enforcement.

It is also part my journey to help LEOs confidently prepare themselves to be the best guardians possible. Officers must first know who they are, then understand their role and how to perform the tasks they are given, to the best of their individual abilities.

Successful policing is performed by confident police officers.

Successful police officers understand and are able to carry out their responsibilities in a competent, confident manner. And with sincere intent to do right and do good.

Training, teaching, and talking with thousands of officers from all geographical locations and demographics has given me the following insight. As the general public, and as police administrators, we expect way more from our police officers than we are willing to prepare them to handle. One more time for those in the back row:
We expect way more from our police officers than we are willing to prepare them to handle.

Expect Less

As a society, we expect our LEOs to be EMTs, substance abuse counselors, family counselors, juvenile counselors, psychologists and/or psychiatrists, as well as roadside mechanics, law enforcers, and to solve any other problems we cannot handle ourselves. LEOs are the utility players on the team. The catch-all.

We expect officers to perform these jobs flawlessly, though many of these roles require advanced learning degrees and hundreds of hours of clinical training.

When I worked patrol, there were several times I received a call from a psychiatrist, psychologist, or mental health professional asking me to go to a place and meet with their client to determine the necessity of an involuntary mental health evaluation, or a forced commitment to a mental health facility or hospital. Let me sum it up.

I, a police officer with zero formal training, was being asked by a doctor of psychiatry (PhD), to evaluate a patient they have been seeing to determine if the patient needed their freedoms and liberties stripped away by the government (aka me). Where does that make any sense?

On one particular call I responded with two counselors to a residence concerning a female patient who was quite depressed. She hadn't eaten or drank any fluids in over a day. She was dehydrated and needed physical medical help as well as psychological help. I listened to the paramedics describe her dire physical state.
They said she needed fluids, like, yesterday. They described how her kidneys were shutting down and she was going to suffer long term problems. Based on this information, I expected the MH workers to compel her to go to the hospital.

One MH worker started trying to make a deal with her. They went back and forth for about 20 minutes. The counselor finally told the patient that she just needed to go. To which the patient countered with, "how about I just stay home until tomorrow and if I still feel bad, I will head in on my own?"

To which the two MH workers conferred off to the side for a moment, and came back with, "Ok. That sounds reasonable."

Wait! What?!

They were willing to let the patient, who hadn't taken in any food or fluids in days, decide the outcome of the situation. I didn't see her as being the best self-advocate or personal decision maker right then. I didn't think the MH workers were doing any better.

Doubting the patient's actual intent to follow through, I stepped in. I was there to help the patient, so I helped the patient. The exchange went something like this.

> Me: "Umm, in principle that does sound great. However, let's do it this way. If you go to the hospital now, and the doctor says you are ok to come straight back home, I will drive you back home immediately."
>
> She:*side eye glance* "How about if I just stay here today, and go in on my own tomorrow? I will even call you to let you know I am going in."
>
> Me: *points finger at her* "That is an excellent idea. However, I will not be working tomorrow. If you are in great shape right now, you will have no problem convincing the doctors to let you go home. Then you will have the proof you need to make us leave you alone. Without a doctor telling us to, we cannot and will not leave you alone right now."

Eventually she agreed to go to the hospital. I believe she thought she could bamboozle the doctors. She didn't. While they treated her for dehydration, they determined she needed a 72-hour mental health hold.

Even with no formal training I was able to understand her angle and her deflection methods and work around them. I also felt like I was more considerate of the need to help her and overcome her resistance than the actual MH workers.

I realize that not every officer is able to see situations in this way. I knew and know of many officers who would not feel confident enough to override the MH professional, even if they might not be serving the patient's best interest. I fell back on "what is my goal?"

My goal was to help her through her current situation. I actually applied the Safety Priorities to the situation (We will discuss these later). I viewed her as a victim or hostage of herself. So, I rescued her from herself, if that makes sense.

Police officers are supposed to talk a suicidal person out of self-harm, then run down an armed robber, while administering Narcan to an overdosing heroin addict. We are "trained" to be psychiatrists, ER doctors, etc., and with the time remaining, law enforcers and peace officers.

This expectation comes with maybe 10 hours a year of formal training in the non-LE fields. But we are expected to be 100% effective. Compare this expectation to Major League Baseball batting averages.

The 2019 MBL batting championship winner and runner up had .335(AL) and .329(NL) batting averages. The American League 2019 winner's batting average dropped from .335 in 2019 to .321 in 2020, yet he negotiated a new 6-year salary contract of **$25M, with $4M annually**.

The 2019 second place batter's average dropped 30% from .329 in 2019 to .205 for 2020. His salary is a mind-boggling 7-year **$188M guaranteed, with $26M annually** [17]!

Nobody asked either of them to give any of that money back or talked about defunding Major League Baseball.

To put this into perspective, I know police officers in this country, today in 2021, who are working for less than what some people make in fast food. I saw a tweet that asked why police officers can't deescalate situations as well as people working at a 24/7 McDonald's restaurant?

An answer was, "Because we get fired if we don't."

I thought, "pay your police as much as you pay your McDonald's employees, and you may get better effort and more accountability."

The lowest 10 states pay their police officers less than $50,000 per year [18]. Don't get caught up in "but the cost of living…" A car costs the same everywhere. Gas and food are similar across the country.

A recent ad for new officers in a small town in MS listed the starting salary of $32K. That is $16/hr. to make life and death decisions, not make sure the pickles go on top of the tomato.

The starting salary for an NYPD police officer is $42,500/year, according to the NYC government website. That is $21.25/hour, pretax, to provide the service expected of a police officer. While trying to live in or around New York City.

I am constantly impressed at the high quality of policing in areas where they don't value their law enforcement as much as their Value Meal.

The effort of law enforcement in these towns and cities is a testament to the dedication to service by a group of people who are vastly undervalued by their communities. We should not base the officer's salary on the cost of living.

A police officer's compensation should be based on the value and level of service we expect or require from them.

And waving thin blue line flags while shouting, "Back the Blue!" doesn't pay anyone's mortgage or feed their children.

We pay police officers less than $40K a year to protect us from predators, to save us when we overdose, to talk us down off a ledge, etc. We want to pay discount prices for our safety, but we expect top dollar performance.

Conversely, we happily pay a grown man who entertains us with a child's game $188 MILLION DOLLARS to hit a baseball ball 3 out of 10 times!

If your comeback is, "kids can't play baseball like major leaguers.", my answer is, "Then don't expect major league law enforcement from your police officers if you are going to pay them a child's allowance.

When we won't invest in a critical need like public safety, yet spend well beyond our means for entertainment, we are explicitly illustrating what is important to us. The public is proclaiming with their wallet what they value.

It isn't their safety.

Require More

Over the years we have added more and more expectations, tasks, and responsibilities to police officers. While increasing the expectations of the job, we have also lowered our requirements.

We have stopped requiring our LEOs to be considerate, fearless, accountable, and all those other great traits. We allow our LEOs to shoot 12-year-old children playing in the park and call it a tragic accident [19].

We allow our officers to berate, humiliate, target, and otherwise intimidate whole communities through drug interdiction, and excuse it as “law and order”, “targeted enforcement”, and "crime suppression".

Crime suppression shouldn't feel like community oppression.

We talk about holding our officers accountable when and if they should do wrong, then we say they never do wrong; even as they do wrong.

We have reached new lows when a police officer, serving a “high risk” no-knock narcotic warrant on a third-party residence based on weeks old information, shoots blindly into the residence killing one of the occupants and we spread false accusations about the woman killed instead of requiring law enforcement to look at themselves.[20].

We don’t have any requirement that the detectives use modern decision-making principles and tactics. We have no requirements that they could have done a better job planning and serving the warrant with care for the residents' safety.

We have no requirement that, prior to shooting dozens of bullets into an occupied structure, the responsibility for controlling the situation rested with the police who inserted themselves into the lives of the scared, untrained residents.

We put more requirements on the public to “make split second decisions in a rapidly changing environment” with greater accuracy than we put on the trained professionals.

Police administrators expect officers to do more with less. They reduce training time for police related job functions, defensive and arrest tactics, firearms and firearm decision-making (that's not important...), and training in basic interpersonal communication.

We have lowered requirements on officer performance because we know they are not trained well enough to competently do any of the dozens of jobs we expect them to do.

They can't possibly have enough time to prepare, train, then perform their duties to our expected level of performance. Think about the baseball analogy.

MLB players get hundreds of training time hours with a hope that they will perform at 30%. Police officers get a couple hours of training time and are expected to perform at 100%. Where our sports teams are well supported, our public safety is an afterthought.

We set up our law enforcement officers for failure and then we act surprised when they fail.

A common misconception held by the public and policing alike is that with more training we are better trained. This approach of "a lot of a little bit of" training is not developing officer preparedness. It is developing anxious officers who are underprepared and overwhelmed.

We must take some of the tasks, responsibilities, and expectations off the plate of law enforcement. And we must be required to do better at our jobs and interactions, especially prior to using lethal force.

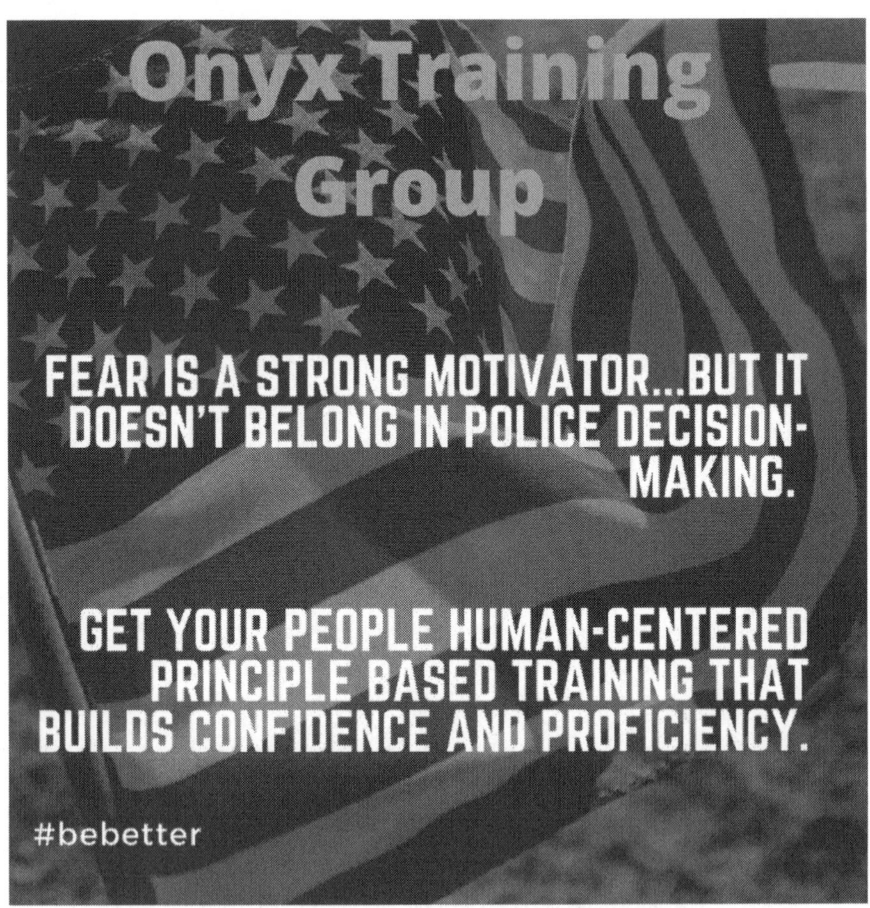

A shameless plug for high quality police training.

6: The First Step to Restoring Relationships

"Stop Talking already..."

In Mesa, AZ Daniel Shaver was called in to the police as a person holding a rifle in a hotel room. I do not know what he was doing with the rifle other than showing it to a friend. Police responded and were able to contact the people in Daniel's room.

Body Worn Camera (BWC) video recorded the encounter, video released showed the relevant portion, approximately 5 minutes.

As Daniel and an unnamed female exited the room, they were told to kneel down then lie prone on the floor of the hall. The officer, who I will refer to as the shooter told Daniel to place his hands on his head and not move or "You will be shot!"

He also gave Daniel very specific directions, each time, telling Daniel to follow them exactly or he would be shot. The female was taken into custody. During this 2-minute portion, Daniel could be seen crying and heard begging the shooter not to shoot him.

Daniel appeared to be mildly intoxicated. He also appeared to work really hard to concentrate on performing the instructions correctly. He seemed to grasp that failing this test could prove costly.

After the female was taken into custody, the shooter told Daniel to come up to a kneeling position. He told Daniel to crawl on his knees towards the officers. He told Daniel that if Daniel fell while crawling on his knees to not put his hands out to break his fall, but to fall on his face.

The shooter told Daniel to not try to pull up his shorts if they fell down. When I say telling I mean screaming. All these instructions are screamed at Daniel in an anxiety producing volume of speech. Each instruction ended with "or you will be shot".

As Daniel crawled on his knees, intoxicated, scared, and performing unpracticed actions, he started to fall. He caught himself, but his shorts also started to come down. Resorting to his unconscious practice and social etiquette, he reached back to pull them up.

The shooter shot Daniel 5 times, killing him right there.

When did Daniel not comply with the shooter?

Daniel did everything the shooter told him to do for 5 solid minutes, including placing his left foot over his right while lying down. Daniel made an unconscious movement to avoid embarrassment in an extremely stressful situation.

It should not be, "if at any time, during the in-custody process the suspect doesn't do exactly as we say, the exact way we say it, we get to kill them."

Compliance is not be a fatal game of "Simon Says".

Personal Connection: To help understand the ripple effect and how we are all connected. I was teaching a class in the south, and we were talking about this tragedy. One student said, "Daniel Shaver was engaged to my cousin. He was an exterminator and was showing his friends his air rifle used to exterminate rodents. It wasn't a real rifle. Both families are devastated."

Just comply...

In many use-of-force incidents we fall back on the excuse that "they should just do what the police said." What about when the person is compliant, and police still shoot and kill them, or injure them? What is the justification then?

Sometimes in policing we distance ourselves from disturbing events by thinking "nobody I know would be in that position."

We are not in some far-off land, conducting war against foreign enemies. We may be down the street from our house, or the person involved may be somehow related to us or other officers. And absolutely people we know, including ourselves, could be "in that position".

We work with and for our fellow countrymen. George Floyd was killed while lying on the ground, handcuffed. He begged for his life, telling his killer that he was dying. He even called out for his long dead mother!

(Floyd was 6'7"/260 and they were going to put him in the back of an Explorer. I am not that big, and I do not fit in those back seats. And if you don't think his race, combined with his size factored into the officers' response, you haven't been paying attention)

Yes, he was a convicted criminal.
Yes, he once held a gun to the belly of a pregnant woman.
Yes, he was under the influence of some narcotic.
Yes, he struggled with police prior to begin put on the ground.
Yes, he was not a model citizen.
Yes, I doubt I would want to hang around him.

But he was not noncompliant for the 8 minutes and 46 seconds a police officer knelt on his throat and two other officers knelt on the rest of his body. He was in handcuffs, crying as his life was taken, all captured on video. It's hard to paint him as culpable for his own death when he is crying and begging to not be killed for over 8 minutes.

And, beyond all, George Floyd was a *human being*.

Philando Castile was stopped because he "fit the description" of an armed robbery suspect. When contacted by Officer G. Yanez, Castille told Yanez he was a concealed carry permit holder who was armed. This is textbook compliance.

The officer asked for Castile's identification, vehicle paperwork and told Castile to not reach for his gun. Castile, again in total compliance, told Yanez he was reaching for his wallet, not his gun as he reached toward his right hip.

Yanez suddenly began screaming at Castile to not reach for his gun. Castile tried to reassure Yanez, but Yanez was already in condition black, not thinking, not listening. He was reacting to some unsubstantiated perception created in his own mind.

Yanez shot Castile 7 times at point blank range, as Castile's girlfriend sat next to him, and his young daughter sat directly behind him. In a twisted bit of consolation, all the bullets stayed in Castile, shielding his daughter from harm.

Too many people, disproportionately minorities, have been killed doing exactly what an officer told them to do.

These tragic events involve a component of race, but they are far more examples of the defective, fear-based training that has taken over how we prepare police. Fear-based inoculation training was directly cited in the Castile case, prompting Yanez' agency and other agencies to discontinue sending their officers to such training.

As a trainer watching these videos, hearing the words, and observing the actions of the officers, I lay the blame at the feet of us trainers, who have trained our officers to shoot first and don't even worry about asking any questions.

No Excuse for Bad Policing

> "the words of truth are simple, and justice needs no subtle interpretations, for it has a fitness in itself; but the words of injustice, being rotten in themselves, require clever treatment."
>
> –Euripides, from
> Thomas Jefferson's

This profession is based on telling the truth and telling it simply and accurately. The truth needs no "massaging or articulating". It just is. I always say, "It isn't what you can "articulate". It's what happened."

When we make excuses and spend more time rationalizing bad behavior than working to improve our profession, we send a bad message to the public. We tell them their concerns are invalid, and we discount and dismiss them.

The public are our customers.

It would be like buying a gun that didn't shoot straight because the sights were off. You tell the manufacturer about the defect or problem. The manufacturer tells you that you are wrong. But you and several others have experienced the sight malfunction.

Even though the other customers corroborate your story, the manufacturer denies the validity of your complaint, eventually saying everything is fine. You just need to aim differently.
Accept the flaw of the gun.

A flaw that can be fixed, but it means the manufacturer would need to acknowledge they made the gun wrong and change the way they built the gun. Make fundamental changes. Would you feel you had a legitimate complaint and were being wrongly dismissed?

Should you change your beliefs and actions (how gun sights function) to accommodate the manufacturer's unwillingness to change what you, the customer, perceive as a serious and dangerous product design/construction flaw?

Our customers are telling us, they perceive a problem with the product or service. If we don't listen and make changes ourselves, the public will make the changes for us.

In late 2020, a District judge in Northern Colorado wrote a 17-page ruling outlining why she agreed with the District Attorney who will no longer accept a certain police officer as a key witness in any case brought before the court.

She agreed with the assessment that this officer is a "danger to the community". The District Attorney called this officer "damaged goods".

This officer was acquitted of manslaughter in 2020 after being charged in 2019 for shooting and killing an unarmed man walking towards him, evidently in a provocative manner.

According to the judge's writings, the officer, in other events, displayed actions and decision-making contradictory to other officers on scene, unnecessarily escalating a situation and jeopardizing the people involved.

When a judge and DA call you "damaged goods" and "a danger to the community" you are not seen as a sheepdog. You are not considered a guardian. You are a wolf.

In 2019, the State of California passed a bill changing an officers' ability to use force from "reasonable force to necessary force for the circumstance".

This now allows for after-the-fact determinations in such cases as a person using a facsimile weapon to provoke officers to shoot them. Or increased scrutiny in an incident where a suspect is physically beating an officer, but only using "personal weapons" (fists and feet).

I have long said if we are not responsible with our decision making, our decisions will be made for us by people who have no understanding of our decision-making needs.

Stop Blaming the Victim

"George Floyd shouldn't have died like that, but he had a criminal history, and he pointed a gun at a pregnant woman's belly once, several years ago." "

Breonna Taylor was involved in drugs, and her boyfriend was a drug dealer." (This smear statement is not only a deflection, but also verifiably false. But it is still being pushed almost a year later)

"They should have just done what the officer told them to do." (My favorite ignorant cliché)

These are all examples of victim blaming. You may not think George Floyd is a victim, but he is. The criminal charge against Derek Chauvin says so.

You may think that Breonna Taylor was somehow responsible for a police officer firing blindly into her apartment, killing her. But she wasn't.

When we lay blame on people who are victims we are only trying to excuse, rationalize, deflect, and justify extremely poor behavior and decision-making, as well as gross negligence on the part of law enforcement.

If you want to put responsibility for incident resolution on the people who caused the problem in the first place, do not get upset that the police/community relationship doesn't improve.

If we are going to blame others, but also will not account for our own poor actions, we should shut up and be content that less than half of the public even wants law enforcement around.

In blaming others for our actions, we take away our ability to be in control of ourselves and influence a successful outcome. We take away our power and ability to make changes.

I acknowledge the suspect always has a say in the outcome. They do. We plan our actions and resolutions with the potential actions of the suspect in mind.

We also plan with contingencies, so that if a suspect does take an action, we already have in place a flow chart of responses to counter those actions and bring control of the situation back towards us.

We must stop blaming the "other" in every case where police officers use excessive or obviously questionable force against the public. We must stop giving police officers more allowances and acceptance to make mistakes or be wrong than we give the public.

"What about Chicago, or BLM?"

During the Protest Summer of 2020, we heard this familiar cry/question any time the Black Lives Matter Organization condemned a police shooting or some other incident of perceived excessive force.

People took to social media and asked the question, "Why doesn't BLM care about Black-on-Black crime, like in Chicago?"

As I thought about this perspective that appeared to make sense on the surface, I realized how flawed it is. Yes, BLM should definitely be concerned with the amount of Black people being killed by other Black people. If they want Black lives to be safer, to matter more, as an organization, they should work to make them matter to both white people and Black people, yes.

But why might BLM be more upset about Black people being killed by police than by other Black people who happen to be street criminals, gang members, or even just family members and friends?

What possible reason could there be for people to be more shocked and upset that the people who swore an oath to uphold the law and protect ALL people, equally, are killing you?

Could it be people expect a higher level of consideration, a higher level of accountability, a higher value on human life, from police than they expect from drug dealers, gang members, and violent street criminals?

Perhaps they just expect police officers to act like better human beings. It could very well be the public just expects or at least wishes its police officers to be more value-based, human being considerate, and more life-preserving than they expect criminals to be.

Before you fall back to the debunked argument about police not shooting Black people in greater numbers than they do white people, etc., remember the statistics I showed you. Black people, by percentage of population, are almost 3 times more likely to be killed by police than are white people.

There is a quantifiable difference in the way police interact with Black people than they interact white people. Facts vs. feelings. This data includes all people, but it is still simple math that all things being equal, percentage wise, police are shooting more unarmed, nonthreatening black people than unarmed, nonthreatening white people.

If you believe the police should be no more scrutinized and critiqued than gang members and criminals, you are saying that police should not be expected or required to act any better than gang members and criminals.

This mentality says law enforcement officers need not be held accountable to the very laws and standards they uphold, and to which they require others to be accountable.

You are promoting the acceptance, and supporting, that police officers be allowed to abuse and terrorize the public like criminals do, with the same disregard for human life, Constitutional rights, and laws.

I will never, never, never accept law enforcement be allowed to operate with a level of accountability and dedication to preservation of life equal to violent criminals.

Ever.

7: The True Role of Policing

"It's not a barrel roll"

At one time, police officers wanted to be associated with the famous Norman Rockwell painting of the police officer and the runaway at the ice cream counter. The long-time image of the police officer as the one person a child can go to for help without question and know that they will be safe. We should still want that.

We used to want to be Austin, TX Police Officer Ramiro Martinez, who climbed the Clock Tower at the University of Texas in 1966 and stopped a murderous rampage. Even in the late 90's, when I got into SWAT, the police response in this event was held up as an example of being a true guardian, or sheepdog protecting the flock.

Today, officers want to be the Punisher, a fictional comic book character who acts extrajudicially and without the rules and laws that prevent law enforcement from really "taking out the trash".

The Punisher doesn't follow laws, policy, or procedure, but it's ok because he is ridding the streets of criminals and "bad guys". Never mind that the Punisher doesn't like police officers or law enforcement. He thinks they are corrupt and useless.

Perhaps we should get back to emulating real-life heroes and stop aspiring to be fictional antiheroes.

Public Image Overhaul

Law enforcement needs to be believed again, to be trusted again. We have squandered the public trust by falsifying reports, planting evidence, and coercing confessions from innocent teenagers (Central Park Five).

WE have tarnished the badge ourselves, nobody did it for us.

And to all those officers who say, "I do the right thing. I'm not one of the bad cops." I hear you. I believe you. Let me ask you...

Beyond writing your tickets legibly and beyond appearing for court in a suit or your class A's early and without complaining, "What are you doing to actively portray policing in a positive light?"

How are you positively interacting with your community in a nonenforcement capacity?

If you are doing amazing things, I applaud you. This part isn't about you. It's about the small percentage of officers who are ruining the image of policing and/or killing citizens.

Rebuilding our public image and public trust isn't about being a great enforcer of the law. It isn't about writing everyone tickets because you don't play favorites. You get no brownie points for being a great Robo-cop.

We need the "Andy Griffiths" now. We need the “officer friendly” who will talk to people just because they acknowledge them as fellow human beings. The community needs the Norman Rockwell officer who will enjoy a soda with the runaway kid, then walk them back home because they know where their family lives.

The community needs its police to stop being The Punisher and start being Guardians.

If we work at being human to other humans, we will create and build a new paradigm. We will cause a shift in how we see the public, and how the public sees us. This is a generational endeavor. Things won’t change dramatically over night.

Law enforcement isn't responsible for changing the overall societal mindset or paradigm. That mindset is society wide, and only society will effect that change. But now that we are aware it, we can shift *our* perspective.

We can take a moment to pause when we are about to ask that young minority person for consent to search them or their vehicle because we think they are acting “hinckey” so they must have dope in the car or on their person.

What does “hinckey” even mean? Sure, it may mean acting sketchy or guilty, but it has become more of a catch-all phrase that really means acting “not like me”.

We can realize that someone looking at you "with a shocked look" isn't probable cause to contact, fight with, arrest, and jail them for...resisting arrest. (Chicago PD February 2021)

Maybe we also ask ourselves why we didn't ask to search the vehicles of the last 10 white people, especially the 65-year- old lady who kept complaining that she was only speeding because she was late to a donor meeting at the opera.

We must start changing our society by changing ourselves. And only ourselves. We have no control over others. But we can be a worthy example to others and model a change they may then choose to make in themselves.

I hear officers around the country complain about this very difficult change. They say policing will never be 100% accepted. People don't want to be held accountable so they will always hate police. It's not the police who need to be retrained, it's the public. I call BS.

We do not control the public. But they are not the trained professionals. They didn't take on the role of police officer in their community. They weren't the ones who said, "I will deal with the wolves. I will be the guardian of this flock."

It is a deflection, and lazy, to lay the responsibility for being mature, professional, compliant, and accountable at the feet of people who are calling for your help because they have utterly no idea how to be any of those things.

At best, it is naïve to believe the people who created the chaos or live in the chaos, can "just stop" and suddenly be reasonable. If they could do that you wouldn't have a job.

We in policing should aspire and strive to be that example of voluntary compliance, character, integrity, and accountability we expect from our other community members. How can we not hold ourselves to high standards, yet require such from others?

When we get called out as a profession, we need to do different and do better than just deflect and point fingers at people who never swore an oath to be of strong moral character, high values, and to impartially serve in the role of public peacekeeper.

I am not saying the law enforcement profession is bankrupt. Far from it. I know there is an overwhelming amount of police officers who show up every day, ready to do the best job they know how to do. I just want them to be seen, so we need to get rid of the ones wreaking havoc and killing our customers.

The Role of Policing

"The role of policing is to create, grow, and sustain positive relationships."

Yes, police write tickets, take people to jail, help people work out differences, and hold people accountable when they wrong their neighbor. These job tasks are all part of a bigger picture. They are not goals, in themselves.

The end goal of these tasks or job responsibilities is community relationship building and growth. Everything police do is to affirm how voluntary compliance with written laws and natural laws enhances our quality of living with others, by strengthening positive relationships among strangers who otherwise have no connection.

Police officers are the physical embodiment of the law.

Laws are abstract words on paper. Law enforcement officers bring those laws to life, in either a positive way or negative way, depending on the officer's embrace and portrayal of compliance.

The public sees a confusing double standard that too often does not hold LEOs accountable to the same level as the public. We should understand how reasonable this confusion and frustration is to them.

We help the public get along with each other. We hold people accountable to their neighbors and fellow human beings. When someone wrongs their neighbor, we help serve as a reminder to them, and the whole group, of the importance in observing other people's rights and liberties.

We encourage, expect, we require people to coexist peacefully and to work out differences in acceptable manners and through the proper channels. Law enforcement must be bound by the same laws, expectations, and requirements as everyone else.

Understanding that all police actions are strategies to achieve the main goal of creating and growing positive relationships, we can better understand how our efforts match or contradict our intent. To me, law enforcement has lost the role of policing.

We have over processed and over systemized this profession to the point where we are schizophrenic and confused about how to fulfill our role. We feel that heaping more jobs or tasks on officers will improve connection with the public, increase officer investment, and help restore public trust. But it isn't working.

We have set apart our officers on an elitist pedestal, discouraging partnerships and collaborations with other community/governmental service providers while declaring our officers to be subject matter experts in everything. But we've done this without giving them adequate preparation, training, and support.

The greatest disservice we have done to our police officers, and our community, is to continue to do one thing while claiming to be doing something very different.

We develop our officers to be fearful, distrustful, and skeptical of the public, while telling the public that police officers are selflessly dedicated to providing the best public safety possible.

Because of this trained-in fear of the public, law enforcement's actions of shooting children [21], raiding the wrong house on warrants [22],[23], killing nonthreatening suspects [24],[25], and killing innocent people [26], have made the public increasingly fearful, distrusting, and skeptical of the profession.

Working with a small police agency in Colorado. Over 80% of police agencies in the United States have fewer than 30 officers.

8: Growing Guardians

"What you plant, will grow"

To be effective police officers we must know who we are as individual people, then what we are as a group. Let me start with an analogy all LEOs understand. The sheep, the wolves, and the sheepdogs.

As far as I know this was conceived by a Vietnam veteran and told to former Army officer and now nationally recognized police trainer Lt Col. Dave Grossman a long time ago. Grossman popularized this analogy. I first heard it in 1992. It goes like this:

You have three groups of people; the sheep are the community members, like a flock. The wolves are the predatory criminals who harm the sheep. The sheepdogs are the LEOs who protect the flock. They watch out for, and work to prevent the wolves from harming the flock. Pretty simple. I have done some updating and added nuances to the scenario.

The sheepdogs have a hard time protecting the sheep because they roam in a big open area. The wolves are quick and sneaky and don't play by any rules. They can do whatever they want.

The sheepdogs are outnumbered. No matter what the sheepdogs do, they keep losing sheep. The shepherd gets upset and beats the sheepdogs.

The sheepdogs decide it is too hard to watch all the sheep from within the flock, so they move away from the flock, up the hill to the edge of the trees. Being on the edge of the dangerous forest, the sheepdogs also need to protect each other from wolf attacks and other dangers lurking in the forest.

The emphasis becomes self-safety and fellow sheepdog safety. The flock's safety becomes less important.

The wolves befriend the sheep. They don't do wolf things all the time, so the sheep become comfortable with them. The wolves act almost like sheep much of the time. As with all predators, the wolves find it easier if they take time to pick out the weakest sheep in the herd. Not all sheep make good victims.

Meanwhile, the sheepdogs, sitting up on the hill, away from the flock, become less familiar to the sheep, even becoming strangers. The sheep become more comfortable with the wolves than with the sheepdogs.

Because the sheepdogs have been thinking like wolves in order to outsmart them, they now appear to the sheep to have wolfish behaviors. The sheepdogs don't appear friendly anymore. They scare the sheep more than the wolves do.

Periodically the sheepdogs run down the hill into the flock when they discover a wolf disguised as a sheep. But sometimes, they strike real sheep, mistaking them for wolves in disguise. The sheep get upset with the mistaken identity.

Now they really don't like the sheepdogs because the sheepdogs are falsely accusing some of the sheep of being wolves. Plus, the sheepdogs only come around to nip at the sheep's' heels to keep them in line.

The sheepdogs are confused because they think they are doing a great job. They think they are keeping the sheep safe from the wolves. Why can't these stupid sheep realize that?

Why can't they realize how much danger the sheepdogs are placing themselves in by living in the fringe at the edge of the dark dangerous forest?

The sheepdogs have placed themselves on the thin blue line of danger and the dumb, ungrateful sheep don't appreciate it!

The sheep agree that the sheepdogs are more dangerous to the sheep than the wolves. They end up helping the wolves more than they help the sheepdogs. The sheep aren't committing crimes, but now think they understand why the wolves don't like the sheepdogs either.

Frustrated by this lack of appreciation and understanding, the sheepdogs nip a little more often at the sheep, even just barking in their faces for no real reason.

And here we are.

We are now in a time where the sheep are more comfortable with the wolves than with the sheepdogs. Because they have focused on the wolves, the sheepdogs have become more like the wolves to the sheep than the wolves themselves.

The sheepdogs, who believe they are still the same as they always have been, are frustrated that the sheep seem upset with the sheepdogs and comfortable with the wolves.

The sheepdogs started down the wrong road when they moved away from the flock and focused on the wolves more than the sheep. They should have stayed among the sheep and built positive, ongoing relationships with the sheep.

Had the sheepdogs stayed among the sheep, they would have been seen similar to the sheep, but with a special ability to protect. They would have been seen as protectors, not only as enforcers, invaders, or occupying forces. How do we fix this?

We shift from warriors to Guardians.

When police officers use the words "war" and "warrior", "fight" and "battle" to describe what we do in our communities, we create a picture and mindset that will not develop the relationships we want. Words matter.

By calling ourselves Guardians we create a mindset that we are guarding our community, protecting it and everyone inside. When we consider ourselves protectors and part of the group, we will focus on the community. We will remain among the sheep, identifying with them more than with the wolves. The sheep will recognize us as part of the group.

As LEOs we must also remind ourselves that the main goal is to build a strong community, not only fight the wolves.

We are sheepdogs, not wolfhounds.

I first attended a Lt. Col Dave Grossman seminar in 1993 or 1994. I will say that not much has changed in his overall speech since then. He has updated some specific cases and some quotes, but he hasn't changed it much. Why not?

Because he doesn't need to!

Timelessly relevant information is just that. Timeless and eternally relevant. There is no need to alter it, just pass it on to the next generation. I consider my perspective much the same. It is timelessly relevant. It doesn't have a shelf life.

I do not agree with everything Lt. Col. Grossman says, but that is ok. We have the same overarching idea about the purpose, the role, and the goal of police officers. We express it using different words based on our experiences and frames of reference.

Grossman uses the term warrior much in the way I use Guardian. Grossman has a military background, mine is civilian policing only. I do not use the term warrior for specific reasons. I teach civilian police officers to consider themselves as Guardians not warriors.

A warrior seeks to be at war. It is what they train for, it is what they understand. In a war, there is one goal, and two sides. There is my side, and my enemy's side. And the goal is to kill and defeat the enemy.

Now that we have been at real war for nearly 20 years, many of our citizens understand war. Many have been to war. When they come home and get hired in law enforcement and we tell them they are "warriors at war", they will reacquire the mentality that probably saved their lives on a battlefield more than once.

But that mentality of ultimate self-preservation, where everybody at the business end of your gun is considered a threat, doesn't always lead to success in civilian policing critical incidents.

There is nothing wrong with being a warrior. We just need to understand how people perceive that label and how they might respond while wearing that mantle while doing civilian policing.

Look at law enforcement and police tactics-related social media and product/service companies today. The line between military (especially special forces) has been so blurred, one can easily mistake a paintball post for a police SWAT post for a Navy SEAL Team post. The dress, physical appearance, and demeanor are all similar.

Many SWAT teams now have changed their body armor to match the type and coverage of military special forces units. This only gives a false perception that civilian police special tactics teams, and officers in general, are soldiers ready for battle. But we are not soldiers.

We are GUARDIANS! Damn, it feels good to be a Guardian!

Think about it. You are the sheepdog of which Grossman speaks. You are the shield of protection for the little old lady who is much more likely to be a victim of crime than a criminal threat to you.

You are the community member who has answered the call, giving to those who need. You have protection skills to give your community. And the people need protecting, sometimes even from themselves.

The Guardian guards. The Guardian protects.

Everybody is under the protection of the Guardian. The warrior doesn't protect, they repel. The warrior hunts. A warrior eliminates the enemy. They go off into the dangerous badlands across the sea, not their own neighborhoods.

The Guardian is among the people right here at home. The Guardian doesn't pick sides or generalize friend or foe. The Guardian must be skilled enough to, "Be nice to everyone but have a plan to kill everyone." as supreme firearms guru Jeff Cooper once said.
A warrior doesn't need to be nice, only to have a plan to kill.

In his book *On Combat* [27], Grossman wrote this about soldiers and police officers who believe violence can be done for good, "When we add the ingredient of discipline with the capability of violence, we create a warrior." I would modify this quote slightly, changing it to, "When we add the ingredient of consideration with the capability of violence, we create a Guardian."

"Competence
matters.
Character mattters more."

–It's Not About You
by
Bob Burg and John David Mann

9: Character, Integrity, Accountability

"The other, other C. I. A."

Right or wrong, I knew it was time to retire when my agency decided to go to body worn cameras. It wasn't because I was worried about being caught on camera doing something wrong. Far from it.

I knew I would never be caught compromising my principles or discrediting myself, my agency, or this wonderful profession. My integrity is too important to do that.

Using illegal or unethical means to catch someone who commits crimes for a living wasn't worth me losing my family's lodging, my income, or my reputation. If they commit crimes today, they will commit them tomorrow. I will prepare better and be ready to catch them next time.

I saw two issues creeping into policing. The first was the public not believing the word of police officers anymore. I noticed a growing disbelief and questioning of LEOs testimony and credibility. And I noticed there was validity to this distrust. That was disheartening.

Second and more disturbing was the lack of trust from police supervision and administration! Though administrators said the move to BWC was to reinforce the officer's statements, which it mostly has done, I saw many instances at my agency, and nationally, where the bosses simply no longer believed the words of their line officers.

It reminded me of the use of replay now is sports. Referees don't worry about making a good call, because they just review the play anyway. I just saw this as a sign that my bosses no longer believed in me and couldn't be the referees anymore.

The officers feel since they are no longer believed, why try? Here is when they begin to damage credibility and trust. Here is when they start nipping at the heels of the sheep and barking in their faces for no reason.

It amazes me how officers are caught violating peoples' rights, falsifying evidence, or perjuring themselves. And it seems always to be over drugs.

Beyond the illegality of it, there is no gain in falsifying evidence in a situation where the person will commit the crime again. And again. If you miss them on Monday, catch them on Thursday.

The act of falsifying evidence and/or testimony is perhaps the least understandable and most reprehensible of criminal activities an officer can commit against a fellow community member. Using one's authority and credibility to provide false witness that a person committed a crime.

If doing this makes sense to you, you have no business being in this profession You are scary. And probably sociopathic.

First, you lied, manufactured evidence, or otherwise just committed a felony.

Second, you did it to convict someone who didn't even commit the crime for which you just committed a crime. How does that make any sense at all?

Third, you didn't solve the crime! The actual perpetrator is still free, and now nobody is looking for them because you made everyone believe you caught the bad guy. But you didn't.

You didn't catch a criminal, you became one.

Character, Integrity, and Accountability

A police officer must have many positive traits, characteristics, and behaviors. But I believe the three main traits or cornerstone traits are Character, Integrity, and Accountability. Without these, officers can become criminals, having no moral compass or firm adherence to right and wrong.

Character is who you are and how you present yourself to others. It is how and what you demonstrate as acceptable and positive ways of living in a community. Character is how you serve as an example of positive behavior and community relationships.

I get it. You don't like some people. That is fine. We all have biases. I definitely do. However, your character is how you operate in spite of those deficiencies and flaws.

Strong positive character is being able set aside your biases and prejudices and treat people fairly across the board. I am not telling anyone to allow themselves to be walked over or to be taken advantage.

If you read into this that I am advocating jeopardizing officer safety, or reducing situational awareness, sign up for one of ONYX Training Group's (my training company) police tactics courses and let's work on critical thinking skills and the development of confidence in your tactical skills. Seriously.

You can be nice to everyone and have a plan to kill them at the same time.

If character is how you present to the world, integrity is how you operate when nobody is looking. Your integrity is an intangible quality that people experience and feel through your character. Your integrity is whether or not you stop at the stop sign when you are the only car at the intersection.

When we commit small transgressions like those above, we build up our tolerance for lying to ourselves. We learn to make excuses and rationalizations that support committing bigger and bigger transgressions (read crimes).

We can now do some pretty slimy things and because our character and integrity have atrophied through rationalization, nothing seems wrong. As long as we are doing it for what we can trick ourselves into believing is "the right reason." We have just become a wolf.

We can lie about a suspect's actions. We can plant drugs in cars, like a deputy in a Florida sheriff's department was recently found to be doing. This deputy's illegal actions created unwarranted humiliation, heartache, job loss, and economic hardships for hundreds of people over a 5-year period. How was he helping his community?

Look at all the people being freed after decades in prison, up to death row, because they didn't commit the crimes for which they were wrongly convicted. That is an absolute tragedy. On EVERY level.

Think about the Houston PD detective in the Pecan Park warrant service shooting who lied to obtain a narcotic search warrant. During the entry a suspect shot four detectives before he and his wife were shot and killed by the fifth officer in the entry group.

Or more recently, the detective who lied in his affidavit to obtain the warrant in the service that ended in Breonna Taylor's killing. There were no drugs in her house because the detective lied about the information that drugs were being delivered there.

Consider the SCOTUS ruling about "the fruits of the poisonous tree" when police violate the 4th amendment. Since the warrant was illegal, everything that happened from the beginning of the warrant service should have been illegal. It doesn't happen every day, but it does happen. And once is too much.

All of these illegal activities have been done by law enforcement officers who did not see their victims as human beings having equal value to themselves.

We, the police, must be accountable, to all and above all.

10: From Fear to Confidence

"Feed confidence, starve fear"

During a podcast [28] interview I was asked by retired police Captain Lawrence Hunter if I was ever nervous and scared right before I would serve warrants. I never was. I was aware. I was conscious of what could happen, and I knew our goal.

For me, much like athletes talk about in sports, time would slow down. Decision making became easier and the right decision, or at least a very good decision, became crystal clear. I know why I felt this way.

My team prepared and trained properly so as to mitigate and manage fear. We used confidence as the cement in our decision making and tactics, instead of using fear as the basis for our decision-making.

Much of police training today tells officers anybody and everybody is a threat. Not even could be a threat. Is a threat. And that everyone are equal threats. We must build officer confidence to help them manage fear.

I once had a student in a tactics class tell me his tactical team made everyone in a house lie face down on the floor when they served warrants. I asked if they even made the suspect's 70-year-old grandmother lie down. He said yes, because a 70-year-old lady could kill him just as easily as a 20-year-old male.

I told him he needed to improve his skills if that were the case. While a 70-year-old lady may be able to kill you, it won't be with an ability equal to a 20-year-old male.

We tell our officers "a weapon in hand is a weapon in play, and everyone is a threat to you."

This is how two Arizona Police officers responding to a noise disturbance call at midnight, shot Ryan Whitacker as he opened his door holding a pistol, not realizing the police were knocking on his door at such a late hour.

Or how an Alabama police officer shot Emantic Bradford Jr., a military veteran, because he was holding his permitted pistol as he was escorting people away from a shopping mall shooting. Afterward, they blamed Bradford for his own death by saying he shouldn't have been holding the gun.

But wait! We police tell the public we need more good guys with guns to stop the bad guys with guns because the trained professionals with guns can't be everywhere all the time.

So, the good guys buy guns...

and we shoot them because we train officers that "a gun in hand, is a gun in play." We are so scared that someone not dressed or looking like us merely has a weapon that we don't even consider their intent.

We aren't even willing to take the time to figure out who are the "good guys".

This is also how uniformed officers shot and killed plainclothes NYPD Detective Brian Simonsen in 2019 during a "friendly fire' incident in a NYC cell phone store. 7 officers fired 42 rounds in 11 seconds. They struck their "targets" (two police detectives and one suspect) less than a half dozen times. We won't even talk about being accountable for every round that leaves your gun.

The suspect was attempting a robbery using a toy handgun. I point out the toy gun to show that the suspect never shot at the police in this event. Only the police shot, and shot, and shot, for 11 seconds. No assessment just panicked shooting and killing a fellow officer, while wounding a second.

How much shooting of fellow officers and innocent people is too much?

How much is acceptable may be the better question. We seem not to have reached our limit.

We don’t train to improve our OODA loop processing ability; we just panic in fear and react in an out-of-control manner.

No, of course, we don’t panic all the time.

If there were only appropriate uses of force, I wouldn’t have written this book. Officers say, “But you only focusing on the bad shootings. There are good shootings too.”

If we only ever had good shootings, we would have no need to train, improve, get better. We really would be the "best we could possibly be". And our relationship with the public wouldn’t be where it is.

However, we are shooting unarmed, nonthreatening, even totally innocent people. We are using inappropriate force against our fellow citizens and community members. We are making poor decisions that cost innocent people their lives.

Police officers literally hold peoples' lives and liberties in their hands.

We must be cognizant of that responsibility. If we are making mistakes that take the lives of innocent people, we need to get better, and I am not going to "hot dog wrap" the pill for you. I am weary of this whole mentality that I can't critique shoddy performance as though policing is some sacred cow. We are creating scared police officers, and they are killing innocent people. Take the damn medicine and get better!

Setting Goals, Building Confidence

Building confidence in police officers begins with teaching officers to understand their goals. Skills and tactics are the strategies by which we achieve our goals. The goals must come first.

You can't even go on vacation if you have no vacation destination goal.

> "I would like to buy a plane ticket."
>
> "To where?"
>
> "I don't know. I just want to buy a ticket."

This doesn't work.

Once we set a goal, we now have a direction our decision-making can travel. No matter what we are doing, we need a goal.

When handling a call, the first thought should be what is the goal here? For the most part it can always start out as "get to the call and figure out what is really going on".

Sometimes, learning of the problem, we realize we don't have any answers. Fear based preparation teaches us to be defensive and deflective. We shrug off the problem and put it back on the citizen.

We do this all the time with "civil calls". When my trainees would try to use that to get out of providing any service, I would stop them.

We may not be able to provide a law enforcement remedy, but we can provide resources to help the person help themselves. These days we can give website links, emails, and other resources to help people navigate uncharted territories.

When people who work in a field that exists to help people don't want to help people, it is usually because they don't know what help to give. They are scared of looking bad. Again, Fear.

Confidence can be realizing you don't know something, admitting you don't know it, and then learning about it. That is what I had my trainees to do.

Sit in the discomfort of not knowing, then get to the business of learning. Think how stellar you look the next time someone needs some obscure resource, and you give it to them because you learned it.

Now you look like a guardian. You have just **increased your confidence** in being able to do a job that is ever changing and morphing, **increased your competence** in doing that job, and **improved the perception of policing** in the eyes of the public.

We set the foundation for our human-centered, principle-based decision making and tactics by developing confidence in ourselves, by learning to manage the fear, and by setting goals for our performance and problem solving.

11: A New Foundation for Police Training

Human-centered, Principle-Based

A Solid Foundation

The first step in changing the way we prepare, train, and support our officers requires setting a solid foundation. Consider defensive tactics. You don't stand with your feet together, but you place them about shoulder width apart, slightly bladed.

On a rookie this looks obvious, but with experience, this becomes more subtle. Still effective, but less noticeable to the public who thinks a bladed standing position is odd.

Our mindset is our stance. It is our initial position. It is how we step into a scene or interaction. It can have a definite impact on our self-confidence, which will impact our self-image and feeling of competence.

We have all seen the insecure officer who only complicates and escalates situations. We all know the officer we don't want to come to our call.

We must first train our officers to remember that every interaction is between humans. LEOs and the public are humans, all with flaws. This is important because some officers see many of the people they interact with as not-quite-as-human as themselves.

Some officers' strong instilled values and belief systems, combined with constantly working with people in crises, or who have more fluid morals or values, can produce a sense of "I'm better than you".

This comes out in generic, debasing terms like "thug", "crack head", "bubba", or other terms people use to establish moral and social hierarchy over other people. "What is in the well, will come up in the bucket."

One of my least favorite terms is people calling white tank top undershirts "wifebeaters". I hate that. It creates a biased presumption against the person wearing the shirt whether we consciously think it or not.

I teach about the Dual Life Value Theory [29]. This was developed by Robert L. Humphrey, a former WW2 Marine Sgt. Humphrey developed the theory that in order to create a positive relationship with someone, one must first see that person as having equal value as a human.

If I can't see you as a person, equal to how I see myself in basic human value, I will never want to have an equal interpersonal relationship with you. I will also treat you poorly since I don't consider you to be on the same basic human level as me.

Military soldiers and first responders actually place the value of other people above their own. They will sacrifice their lives to save or protect others, including strangers. Or at least that is the theory. In practice, we could use some improvement.

But this is the gist of Humphrey's theory. I recommend the book for all first responders. The author developed a vast knowledge base working with different cultures and communities, in a worldwide setting.

If we want to operate to the full measure of our oath of office, we must be willing to put ourselves on the line for others. This includes total strangers, whom we may not consider to be worthy of such sacrifice in any ordinary setting.

In a specific incident, we may need to put our safety in jeopardy for someone we don't agree with or condone. Yesterday's suspect may be tomorrow's victim. I experienced this several times in my career. I fought just as hard to get them justice as I did in bringing them to justice.

> "You must have the same care and concern
> for a stranger as you would a family member."
>
> -Ron McCarthy, Sgt.
> LAPD, LAPD SWAT
> (retired)

Our role is to grow positive relationships. How we think of and consider others has a huge impact in how we develop relationships. If we use negative or derogatory identifiers for individuals, groups of people, or even neighborhood locations, we set a perception of superiority or inferiority. Think of the words you use to describe the different neighborhoods where you work.

Terms like "the hood" or "ghetto" are meant to conjure a certain, negative image. Words like "thug", "crackhead", and "hood rat" are rarely used in a positive way. These types of terms also become racially biased and bigoted code words.
If we allow ourselves to use these words, we allow ourselves to be influenced by our inherent biases. We also present those biases to the world, displaying our bigotries.

Stop using them, even in familiar or casual conversation.

Especially in familiar and casual conversation.

Anchor in humanity

The primary thing to remember is all the people involved in any situation police respond to are human beings. Bottom line. Everyone has the same basic human value and must be given that consideration. This value is aggrandized and exaggerated when we talk about the police as superheroes.

In an effort to promote police quality of effort, competence, and selflessness, we have done the disservice of going the other direction by equating LEOs with superheroes. You know, the whole "not all heroes wear capes" thing. Here is the problem with making this comparison.

What is a superhero?

They are invincible, immortal, unconquerable. They make 100% perfect, split-second decisions, and have lightning quick reflexes. They are always saving the whole world. They are unflappable. They don't get scared.

A superhero isn't a real person.

They are fictional characters. These beings don't exist. We are trying to be cartoon characters.

No matter how hard we work out, how much we bench press (do you even, bro?!), we can never stop a train with our body. We can never swim underwater for extended periods without breathing equipment. We can never fly with just a cape. Squirrel suits are just "falling with style".

The comparison to a superhero puts the real-life police officer in a trick bag. We will never be perfect, but we tell people we are. We call ourselves superheroes, so people expect the Flash, Wonder Woman, or Superman. Then we end up behaving like "Homelander" from *The Boys.*

Maybe if we acknowledged and reaffirmed our humanness, our imperfections, or flaws, the public would be reminded that we are like them. And they might allow for more mistakes.

Law enforcement officers come to work having stayed up all night with sick kids. Police officers have marital problems, financial difficulties, lower back pain, and other human afflictions.

We are inserted into strangers' lives and expected to instantly correct, improve, and repair what may have been decades in the destruction. Sometimes we are having the same problems and don't have answers for ourselves. We may take heroic action in a moment, but we are always human beings.

Law enforcement officers are simply human beings trying to do a tough job the best they can with the life skills they have developed through living and learning as humans on this planet Earth. The people are the police, and the police are the people.

Acknowledging Our "Averageness"

We do ourselves damage when we perpetuate this superhero, superhuman myth by spouting the obviously false statement that "99.9% of police officers are doing a fantastic job and are great examples of quality policing."

I get that this is really just a way to say, "most police are doing a great job" or "the overwhelming majority of police...". But everyone also knows this isn't true. We know this and the public knows this. How?

Because the public interacts with themselves all day every day! Their restaurant orders get messed up. The wrong items get shipped to them. They have all called customer service and computer tech support. LEOs are just people like all other people. We really aren't less flawed than anyone else.

And we, in policing, also know ourselves and each other. We know our colleagues aren't running at 99.9%. So, when we say 99.9% it sounds like a deliberate attempt to deceive the public.

I have talked with officers around the country and various other countries, and (anecdotally) the numbers are more like this:

30-40% doing a very solid to great job. Getting on base almost every at bat or knocking it out of the park, to make the obligatory baseball reference.

50-60% are not messing up too bad. They are getting the job done. In the Police Officer Field Training Program vernacular, they are, at least, minimally acceptable. Nothing to make a movie about, but also not running amok.

@10% or so are the ones lying and cursing on video, wreaking havoc on our communities, and damaging the image of policing. This group includes the grossly inept to the sociopaths, to the criminals with a badge. These officers won't always make the news, but they are the ones fellow officers do not want to show up on their calls. These officers escalate situations, upset the public, and occasionally shoot innocent people.

Those in law enforcement know these numbers are way more accurate. We also have this unfounded fear that if the public heard these numbers, they would lose faith and confidence in policing. News flash! They are losing faith in us now. I don't think admitting we are human, just like everyone else, is going to make things worse.

I think honesty would have the opposite effect. Think of how much more credibility we would have if we were honest with the public. What if we admitted to the public, "We are struggling!"

Believe me, they see the struggle now.

Once we admit we are human, with all the flaws and fears, we can begin to address ourselves, our fellow officers, and then our profession as a whole. As long as we try to maintain this façade of being better than perfect, we will continue to frustrate and confuse the public.

Our actions do not match our words. We all understand that when someone tells you one thing, but does another, like many suspects do under questioning, that person's credibility goes to zero. Why would we expect the public to not consider our credibility based on our words and deeds?

12: The 5 Step Decision Making Process

"One principle to rule them all"

Let's talk about the various concepts that will guide our tactics. Concepts are equal to our thoughts or plans, with tactics being our actions. It is so critical to have solid foundational concepts to guide our actions. As we have talked about, without them we have no understanding of the why of the what.

Why do we want to serve a no-knock warrant in the middle of the night instead of during the day? Do our decision-making principles dictate that to be the most effective course of action? Or is it simply because "that's just how we do it"?

As we discuss the following concepts, consider incidents that have caused outrage, frustration, and pain, and consider how the situation might have ended different if any of these concepts had been used.

All of these concepts I learned back in the mid 1990's so if you come across material in this book that is new to you, ask yourself, better yet ask your police agency why these concepts are not standard practice or common in police training.

I know these principles and tactics work. These tactics have kept me out of multiple shootings (warrant services when the suspect was armed already or gained access to a gun quicker than we could have stopped them) and didn't lose us evidence.

We never cared if we lost drug evidence. Miss them on Monday catch them on Thursday. Loss of dope or other evidence should never supersede the concern for preservation of life, especially in warrant services.

The 5 Step Process

In police advance tactics I teach this process of decision making before any others. If you can only remember one concept, this is the one. It is called the 5 Step Process or the PIE+ process. This decision-making process helps officers make critical decisions based on solid principles and foundations. Here is the "why" of the "what". The process breaks down like this:

Priorities of Life, or Safety Priorities
1)Hostages or victims
2)Bystanders
3)Police Officers
4)suspects

Information/intel/facts
What we know, not what we can possibly imagine

Environment
Where is it taking place?
Indoor, outdoor, summer, winter?

Tools, Tactics, Training

What equipment do we have and how have we learned, and trained, to use it?

Officer Instincts
Based on my experience, how does this feel?

We will greatly increase our proficiency and confidence in our decisions because we are taking into account "why" we are making any decision in the first place. When a SWAT team enters a building, why are they doing it? Is it to rescue a hostage, or simply to find an armed, wanted suspect?

Using this method, we can do much better at ensuring our actions are based on sound reasoning and thought. The first step in this process, as with everything in policing, is the acknowledgement that we are dealing with people. Always people. **Even suspects are people.**

Safety Priorities

We first determine who is involved in the event. Do we have hostages or victims? We must understand that their safety and security are paramount. They are the most important people to consider in any event.

All of our efforts, thoughts and actions, are focused on making victims or hostages safe, getting them help, or getting them justice. Whether this is a hostage rescue or simply working a criminal case, the hostage or victim is who we are working for.

We are not working for our Sgt., our chief, or the POTUS. In the moment we are resolving a critical situation, we are working for the person at the top of the priority list. Also, it is important to remember the person at the top of the list changes depending on the incident, and by the moment.

We don't always have a victim and/or a hostage. Don't get caught thinking we always start with a hostage. Most every case we work will have a victim, but in any crisis event, we must make that determination before taking action. For instance, in a suicidal subject barricade operation there is no victim.

If we have no victim, we then look for innocent bystanders. These are people not in danger but could become part of the problem if we don't prevent it. This is why we establish perimeters around critical incidents. To keep the problem in and the innocent people out. Once they are safe, we think about the officers.

We should not risk officer safety to apprehend a suspect or to keep evidence from being destroyed (there may be instances of national security where we may risk our lives for evidence, but that is rare).

There is no reason to commit to suicide missions to confront a suspect, when nobody else is involved. We have a lot of tools and tactics that can motivate a suspect to surrender.

History has shown that when suspects harm or kill officers, there is rarely a benefit gained by the officer unnecessarily exposing themselves to danger. The suspect either gives up when cornered by superior numbers of officers or they take their own life. Either way would have been accomplished without any officer loss if we observed the Safety Priorities from the beginning of the event.

Finally, after all other groups are safe, we will consider the suspect. They started the dangerous episode, so they are safeguarded last. This is where the use of less lethal resources may come into play.

We will take them into custody but do so from a position of control and resource superiority. This includes noncriminal events like armed and barricaded suicidal people. A suicidal person armed with a weapon is at best a subject, which puts them close to suspect. And below officers. We will not unnecessarily jeopardize an officer's life to save a suicidal person's life [30]. We must continuously ask the question, "Who is at the top of the list now?"

Information/intel/facts

Once we establish the priorities, we consider what we know about the situation. What are our facts?

This is important because without a grounding in the reality of the situation, our minds can make up incredible events. Our minds will create fantasy scenarios that will take us down roads that lead to chaos and tragedy.

Think of Atatiana Jefferson in Fort Worth, TX. A police officer responded to a call from a neighbor saying Jefferson's front door was open at 2am. This is not normal. But on the surface, it is also not criminal. When the officer arrived, he started to consider the possibilities. Not the probabilities, the possibilities.

What was possible in this incident?

1) The wind blew open a door not properly shut
2) A domestic situation that went really bad
3) A burglar
4) A homicidal maniac broke in and was slaughtering everyone inside
5) All of the above
6) None of the above

If we let the possibilities control our actions, we can make up some pretty horrendous scenarios. LEOs must base our actions on the facts or information we do have. That may not be much. We may have very little information. This leaves a lot of uncertainty. Remember how LEOs don't like uncertainty.

We are better off considering the probabilities as our main road to travel. We have contingencies to handle the possible, but we should work in the probable.

The only information the officer had was an open door at 2am. Based on his interpretation of the information he decided he needed to investigate. Not a problem. A solid decision.

But in his mind, he appeared to have decided he was going to find a crime being committed. You may think, "You don't now. You haven't talked to that officer. You can't know what's in his head."

True. But I have either been a policer officer and/or trained police officers for almost 30 years. I have been in his situation many times. As a result of observing thousands of students' actions and quizzing them afterward, I do understand officer thought process.

So, the officer pulled his gun and moved quietly and cautiously around the house. Why did he do this? He did it so he could sneak up on and catch a criminal with his weapon ready if needed. He had no knowledge of a crime being committed, just his perception or belief.

As he walked around outside, he may have cast some shadows, moving slowly, almost lurking among the bushes and shrubs of the yard. His flashlight gave off a small, flickering light.

Atatiana Jefferson, house-sitting in her mother's home, was playing video games with her nephew. She may have seen a light flashing and moving outside, then a figure moving through her yard. Jefferson, without any tactical decision-making training, possibly had her gun to defend herself and her nephew from what she may have reasonably perceived to be a criminal about to break in her house.

As Dean approached the window, his light shone on Atatiana, he saw her gun, and believed he had found his criminal in the process of doing a very bad thing. His senses became overwhelmed, and he panicked. Why do I say he panicked?

BWC recorded video and audio show Dean saw Jefferson in her bedroom holding a gun, screamed, "SHOW ME YOUR HANDS!!!" and shot her immediately. Panic is evident because,

1) He's screaming at the top of his voice.

2) The time between command and shooting was not long enough to allow for Jefferson to comply with his command, even if he intended to let her comply, which he didn't.

3) He obviously saw her hands. She had a gun in one. Why yell "Show me your hands" when it doesn't mean anything? His firearms training and conditioning appeared to have been to always yell that phrase. There is new debate whether this is a good command to yell at all.

4) He's screaming. At the top of his voice.

In Dean's mind he was certain he was looking for, and going to find, a home-invading criminal, and he was going to stop them. Dean's mind took this situation and created imminent jeopardy that he wasn't able to correctly process.

Even being predetermined he was walking into a critical incident Dean was still unprepared to accurately process a response in this incident.

If Dean had responded based on known information, one possibility of many, could have looked like:

1) Dean gets on scene and sees the front door open.

2) He checks on his computer or through dispatch for any recent DV or other disturbance history.

3) He watches the door and residence from a distance for a moment or two, listening.

4) Hearing and seeing nothing, asks dispatch to call inside, if they have a number.

5) Jefferson is contacted inside by phone, she comes out and meets with the officer, she realizes the police do care about her safety, and she makes certain to fully close her door in the future.

6) Steps 4 and up can be changed to no available phone number, Dean cautiously moves to the front door, listening again, then calls inside identifying himself, backs away from the door to a position of cover, and makes contact with Jefferson that way.

Any of these suggested ways, and we are not using this tragedy as a learning example of what not to do, a young lady isn't dead, a young boy isn't traumatized, and a police officer isn't going on trial for criminal homicide, aka murder.

If we base our actions on the information known, we will naturally be more cautious, because we are placing our safety at the top of the priority list.

Whenever we are simply investigating a potential crime, we should start with officer safety at the top of the list. As the situation changes, we may adjust, but until more information comes in, we should proceed cautiously.

The slower we move, literally and figuratively, the more time we give ourselves to make good decisions and not get overwhelmed. (OODA Loop)

Environment

We must consider where the event is happening. In the tactical world, this consideration includes ambient temperature, time of year, time of day or night, location type (house, apartment building, commercial building), or any other factor about when or where something happens that could affect our performance in resolving the situation.

If we return to the Fort Worth scene, we have middle of night, in Texas on October 19, 2019. The recorded temperature was around 54 degrees [31]. Not bad for 2am. The neighborhood is residential, quiet.

The residence is an average sized starter ranch home less than 1500 square feet. The officer could stand outside the house, not be bothered or affected by other people or the cold, listen for abnormal sounds inside the house, and watch most if not all of the important sides of the house (front door, windows, etc.).

Dean's environment supported slowing down to gather additional information before moving forward. We should slow down and gather more and updated information whenever we have the opportunity.

The situation changes with every step, every moment. It doesn't matter what it was like one hour ago, even 10 seconds ago. It matters what it is like now. If we can get current, real time information just prior to taking an action, how can we be better informed than that?

We take action based on the information we have at the time of our action.

Tools, Tactics and Training

Here is where we put together the resources we have, the way we use them and how well we know how to use them.

We need to be aware of the limitations and benefits of our tools/resources. Not everything is effective 100% of the time. It is just as important to know when a tool won't work for you as when it will work.

Police officers need to know how they use their tools, less lethal, etc., especially when in a team. We get used to working alone, making all the decisions. When we work with other officers, the change in dynamics can lead to miscommunication, misperception, and misinterpretation. And then misery.

Training with our tools and with other officers will minimize the confusion in quickly moving critical incidents. But it is crucial that training happen and that it be recurring. We cannot just give officers the tool and an initial training, and kid ourselves into thinking they are well trained.

Jacob Blake

When Jacob Blake was shot 7 times while reaching into, getting into, putting a knife into, whatever you want to say he was doing into his vehicle in Kenosha, WI, we can talk about a break down in tools, tactics, and training.

The officers apparently deployed a taser against Blake as they attempted to get him into custody for an outstanding warrant. However, as many LEOs know from experience, tasers are successful a fraction of the time they are used. There are many conditions that must be met before tasers are 100% effective.

When they work, they work very well. Even when 100% effective, they only incapacitate a person for 5 seconds. After the pulse stops, the person is fully functional. It's not like in the movies. This is not a judgment on the Taser's usefulness. (all tools can be effective in their proper environment) it is an observation of fact.

Having a Taser is better than not having a Taser.

> **My opinion:** The law enforcement profession felt it needed to hard sell mild electrocution to the public, so it touted electronic restraints as the most effective way to subdue a violent suspect without shooting them. Then it oversold the effectiveness, essentially calling Taser a panacea, instead of limited use tool, which it is.

So, the taser wasn't effective. In video of the event, we can see the officers trying to physically subdue Blake with control holds. These holds also prove ineffective. Why?

Training to The Lowest

Police training, contrary to what the public believes, is geared to the lowest functioning officer. It is not some James Bond Movie-Villain-Henchman-Prep School, where physically fit, swarthy complexioned ne'er-do-wells run around shooting targets, dodging flamethrowers, performing flawless hip throws.

Line level police training is more like a bunch of people who thought they had an extra day off but are suddenly told to come into work, and now have to get sweaty in their street clothes. Police defensive tactics and arrest control is practiced by too many officers in a lax mindset, on other officers in a lax mindset.

I'm not saying there aren't officers out there working to be the best they and be. There are very hard-working officers who constantly improve their skills and abilities. There are also many trainers who work very hard to get their students operating at top form.

One of my former coworkers, and a good friend, Jerrod Hardy is a retired police officer and still trains officers in mindset, arrest control, and defensive tactics. Jerrod is a true guardian and grower of guardians. If you desire excellent tactics with a strong foundational base, I suggest scheduling training with his company, Team Hardy. His contact info is in the glossary.

I am saying the overall system is not set up to provide top quality, effective training and preparation for our officers. Much of this deficiency is because of the lack of desire of the end consumer, the individual officer.

Like most officers, the officers in the Blake shooting (illustrated by their actions in a real-life incident) probably trained to apply a less than effective control hold on their training partner, who not wanting to get injured and be on light duty (desk duty) would go along with the deficient hold, pretending it to be effective. This produces poor competency in performance, but the officer doesn't realize that.

A Lesson Learned (side story)

Once, while working in our bar district, I helped with several officers trying to take a man in to custody. I say helped meaning I stood there and watched the crowd, keeping them away from the custody attempt.

I say attempt because three officers were having no success in using several types of control holds or knee strikes to subdue this large Asian man.

I say large, because he was bigger than all the officers trying to subdue him. One officer finally ended the problem by producing his wooden baton.

I say produced because he didn't need to use it. Upon seeing the baton, the large man dropped to one knee and allowed himself to be handcuffed.

After thanking him for such gracious allowance and compliance, an officer asked why he finally stopped resisting. He told them he was a martial arts instructor. No, he was more accurately a Sensei, or very well-qualified teacher.

He said he was aware of all the holds and strikes they attempted on him; he taught them to his students. The problem was the officers were not performing them correctly!

He said if they had done them correctly, he would have been compelled to submit. He dropped to his knee when he saw the baton, because he knew there was no way that would not hurt.

Lesson learned! Thank you, Sensei! (Deep bow)

Nobody told Jacob Blake he was supposed to "go along with the program".

By video evidence and observed actions, he appears to already possess a knife in his hand. And by his actions, he doesn't appear to want to use it against the officers. Why? Because he doesn't use it against the officers.

"Action is a pretty accurate indicator of intent."

Blake appeared, by his actions, to either be intent on putting the knife in his vehicle or putting himself in his vehicle and leaving. The group of officers had no tactics to deal with Blake's actions.

As Blake moved away from the officers, nobody flanked around the back of the vehicle to gain another perspective. They all just walked behind Blake, violating the 21ft rule for knives.

If they knew he had the knife that many officers on social media noticed why would they knowingly violate the gospel rule that you don't allow a person with a knife to come within 21ft of you?

The officers would have been trained on that paradigm. (the rule was increased several years ago to 30-35 ft distance) In all of their training I am fairly certain they were never taught to grab a suspect, holding a knife or not, while holding and pointing their weapon at them. At least I hope they had never been trained that. What could go wrong?!

It's called a sympathetic response. By compressing space and time, while holding a gun in his hand, the officer who shot Blake gave himself too many dilemmas to process and no time in which to process them. When Blake jerked upon being grabbed, the officer flinched, backed up, and squeezed his finger which was on the trigger of his gun.

Looking at the video, the officer appeared to be almost as surprised he shot Blake as I bet Blake was surprised at being shot. When he followed Blake to the driver's door, the officer, by his observed actions, was on overwhelm. He was not responding according to his training, unless that was his training. He reacted out of panic, not reasoned, trained action.

It appeared, by his actions, that all he could think was to not let Blake get away. Whether because of Blake's warrant or some more personal reason, the poorly prepared officer acted out of fear, anxiety, and confusion, not confidence.

I have heard all the rhetoric from those who believe police can do no wrong. I have heard the "Blake had a knife" (I addressed that). I have heard the "he should have just complied".

If we expect a criminal to make good decisions, especially in a crisis situation, who's not thinking in reality?

Criminals make bad decisions for a living.

Blake was a wanted fugitive. He was wanted for a crime he allegedly committed but didn't want to take responsibility for. Why would we expect him to make solid, positive decisions all of a sudden? And, in a crisis situation, no less.

I read an interview Blake recently gave where he talked about having the knife. He acknowledged after the fact that he shouldn't have been holding the knife, but when he saw it drop on the ground after he got tased, his only thought was to put it in his car and not have the officers see it with him or around him. The video evidence actually supports Blake's claims.

As much as we may not want to believe Blake because his actions and thoughts run different to our own, we may do well to not assimilate the information and insight into his thought process, and simply accommodate it. Allow that he may be telling the truth.

Blake never turned toward the officers with the knife. In fact, he kept it close to his stomach, appearing to try to hide it until he tried to put it in his car.

What is evident is that Blake was not making good decisions, but neither were the police officers. But Jacob Blake isn't "highly trained" and doesn't get paid to make tactically sound, life considerate decisions.

We show our naiveté and lack of critical thinking by being shocked that a suspect/criminal would not "just comply" with police commands, a taser, or control holds. We also show our egocentrism and our self-centered view of the world, when we presume everyone should think like us.

We presume everyone thinks, or should think, like we do. Well, they don't. And that is why we, as law enforcement officers, as guardians, protectors, as sheepdogs, must make decisions for everyone involved. We consider the safety priorities and decision-making principles on behalf of people because they have no training or preparation to handle these events.

Once we understand, learn, and ingrain the decision-making process, and other critical principles, we won't put any problem-solving responsibility on the person who created it in the first place. If we are only going to add to the chaos of the situation, it is best we don't show up.

We will take that responsibility on ourselves. For we are the problem solvers. Don't make the person who created the problem responsible for solving it. If they could solve it, they wouldn't have created it in the first place. You have the knowledge, training, and confidence to solve the problem. So, do it.

Officer Instincts

Officers should "listen to their gut". Even accounting for all the prior points, a decision for action still includes how we feel about things. Using our instincts, even just as humans, is what has kept our species in existence for so long. Instinct is a component of our survival system. We need to honor and use it. Animals who don't acknowledge, follow, or even develop their instincts don't last long.

The 5 Step Process accounts for all the basic decision-making considerations that guide the tactics and actions of police officers in critical incidents. This process should be considered the foundation upon which the next principles are laid.

13: Space and Time

"Don't Stand so Close to Me"

Understanding how space, time, and information processing all work together will improve officer performance by increasing confidence, and quality of decision making. This is what people mean when they say that during a critical incident "time seemed to slow down. Everything suddenly became clear."

When we improve our ability to work through problems in natural progression and pace, we increase the opportunities for success. By using space, time, even obstacles to our advantage, we promote better quality critical thinking and decisions.

In the short time it has taken me to write this book, there have been several police shootings. They have ranged from officers being shot at and returning fire, to officers shooting unarmed people simply walking towards them.

In Oklahoma City, 3 police officers shot and killed Bennie Edwards, a local homeless man who was diagnosed as paranoid schizophrenic [32]. Responding to a call of Edwards creating a disturbance at a local strip mall, officers attempted to take Edwards into custody.

Edwards, holding a knife, can be seen on video first trying to move away from officers, then appeared to run towards, then between officers, as they shot and killed him.

In these events, and many others, officers could have greatly changed the outcome if they knew, understood, and applied the concept of space and time.

The more space we have between us and a problem, the more time we give ourselves to work through our resolution options.

With our current mode of training police to fear everyone, or expect everyone to spontaneously and unprovokedly attack, we increase the potential for officers to overact or act inappropriately. If they don't understand space and time and give themselves as much time as possible to make good decisions, officers will compound the potential and inevitability of making poor decisions.

Consider the event in late December 2020 in Columbus, Ohio, where two officers approached a residential garage, responding to a call of a man sitting in a car, turning the engine on and off.

Andre Hill emerged from the garage holding a cell phone. He was shot almost immediately by one of the officers. Hill died at the scene. That officer has since been charged with criminal homicide.

The BWCs show the officers walk right up to the open garage, almost immediately after they arrived. They conducted no assessment from a distance. They made no apparent verbal commands to anyone inside, requesting them to come out, while maintaining a good distance from behind cover. Keep in mind this call was not an emergency or in progress crime.

The call was a suspicious person sitting in a car, in an open garage, running their car, in Columbus, Ohio, in December. Incidentally, the temperature was 30 degree on December 22, the night of this tragedy. Based on the totality of the call, had the police officers employed the simple concept of space and time, Andre Hill would still be alive.

The Dylan Scott shooting wouldn't have happened if deputies had used space and time to alter the decision-making process of the suspect and themselves. They would have simply moved away from the suspect.

This would have changed the suspect's OODA Loop processing which counted on the deputies standing close to him to react to his sudden movements.

Backing away would have also given the deputies a broader view of the overall situation. They would have been able to see more of the suspect had he stepped from the vehicle. This would have allowed for the use of less lethal resources to take the fugitive into custody, with less potential for serious injury.

Distance prevents tunnel focus, or tunnel vision.

Police officers are taught that we should never give up ground we have taken, as though we are an army trying to keep an enemy from a strategic geographical position. I see this in SWAT training. Teams want to hold a position in a house, even when taking fire from an unseen suspect.

I have watched students try to advance on a suspect role player shooting at them, even as they are being hit with the marking rounds (bullets).

As trainers, we must stop training our officers that it is imperative to keep a geographical position at all costs. This mindset is detrimental to our mission almost 100% of the time and violates both the concept of space and time, as well as the Safety Priorities.

When we want our officers to hold a geographical position in any incident absent a hostage or victim, we encourage our officers to put the apprehension of the suspect ahead of their own safety. By staying within striking distance of the suspect our officers also stay within the suspect's OODA Loop.

If we put the apprehension of the suspect above the safety of officers, we should never be surprised when our officers get injured or killed. Getting the Safety Priorities out of order leads to catastrophes.

14: The Suspect Advantage

"I got the drop on ya', Tex!"

In Arizona in 2006, a SWAT team served a warrant against a man selling drugs and illegal weapons. Their intent was to serve a no-knock warrant using dynamic movement upon entry. Their plan was to, in their own words, "use speed, surprise, and violence of action to overwhelm everyone inside and they will have no chance to resist us."

The warrant was documented as part of a national television show called Court TV [33].

The first problem occurred when the explosive breaching charge, or small bomb, placed on the door failed to open the door. I was an explosive breacher. We called that a "bounce". The charge bounced off the object without a positive result.

No police tool is 100% effective, not even explosives.

This "overwhelming" show of speed, surprise, and violence of action resulted in the Team Leader being shot 17 times, with 14 rounds being stopped by his body armor. He was shot in his stomach. He also suffered permanent injury to his hand, requiring him to retire from policing.

The warrant turned into a barricade, with the suspect surrendering without any further shooting. When all was said and done the round count was suspect=40+, SWAT team=0. The action was overwhelming, just not in the way the team expected.

I have seen the post-incident debrief created by the team. The investigation determined the suspect was lying on the living room floor, sleeping next to his semi-automatic rifle equipped with a 100 round drum magazine. He had several other rifles near him.

Being a drug dealer, he was apparently concerned that someone may come try to rob him in the middle of night and he thought the best way to be prepared was to stay near his rifle.

According to their information (#2 in the 5 Step Process), the team knew or believed the suspect had automatic weapons, grenades, and a rocket launcher. Those items were in fact recovered during the search.

This event and near fatal tragedy illustrate the next concept we need to teach our police officers.

The Suspect Always Has Tactical Advantage

I have compiled several real-life police incidents over the years that illustrate this concept. Most resulted in officers being killed or injured. We must remember a few important truths. We do not know the mindset of suspects, their intentions, their level of determination, or their skills.

We don't know what the suspect knows.

A common mistake is a belief that we, the police, are the most prepared, the best trained, the most determined, or the clearest thinking parties involved in the police/suspect interaction.

In the Maricopa "incident", the officers believed that their equipment and tactics would carry the day. They said so in the documentary. As they exited their delivery truck, one of them said, "be ready for a gunfight as soon as we turn the corner."

They did not take into account, or know, that the suspect needed only a basic understanding of space and time, and body positioning, to instantly prevent a dozen well-armed, well protected, highly trained professionals from entering his house.

When we serve a warrant on a house, the suspect knows the house better than we do. They will naturally understand the best location from which to view the entry and exit points (doors and windows), they will know hiding places and can move around furniture to create or block passageways. This gives them a tactical advantage before the incident ever starts.

If hiding in a building, the suspect knows where they are hiding, we must look for them. In the OODA Loop cycle, they can be at the Act phase as soon as they see us coming. We must start in the Observe phase at each moment, or with each new observation.

Think about the incidents that turn tragic and see how often the concept of suspect advantage, is disregarded, unknown, or unaccounted for. The obsolete and deadly refrain from law enforcement and military trainers teaching law enforcement special operations is to "beat the suspect to the gun".

We can never be certain we will beat the suspect to the gun.

Someone thinking about personal safety would naturally keep a weapon near them at all times. Where do most LEOs keep weapons in their houses? Within arm's reach of their beds.

Why do we presume the suspect can't think the same way?

Combine the probability that the suspect is in possession of a weapon before we encounter them, with the understanding that the suspect will be ahead of us in the information process loop, and suspect advantage becomes crucial for police officers to learn, understand, and incorporate into their decision-making.

When police use a plan that combines our tools, tactics, and training, decision making principles, and contingencies, we switch the tactical advantage from the suspect to us. Suspects rarely have a plan B.

Once a suspect's plan fails, they will either give up or, in extreme circumstances take their own lives. Once law enforcement gains the advantage, rarely will a suspect attempt to violently engage them. Contrary to what we teach our officers very few suspects are suicidal or have a death wish.

If suspects don't perceive an opportunity to assault officers and/or escape, the vast majority will give up.

The key words here are perceive an opportunity. If we work smarter, not necessarily faster, they won't see an opportunity. We give them the perception that the best course is surrender.

In one of the first and still most extreme school shootings, at Columbine High School in Colorado in 1999, the shooters, terrorists more accurately, engaged in a gun fight with a school resource officer, or SRO, before retreating back into the school.

They were confronted by the SRO as they were leaving the school, having placed propane bombs in the cafeteria. Once back inside the school, they executed over a dozen students and a teacher, before committing dual suicide without confronting police a second time.

We can conjecture, with reasonable certainty, that the suspects knew encountering the police would not be successful to their plan. They had no issue with shooting unarmed children but weren't willing to get shot at by police.

The post incident investigation determined the suspects' initial intention was, most likely, to set propane bombs and leave the school, surviving the attack. The bombs were intended to do the damage after the suspects got away. Fortunately, the bombs never exploded.

Their retreat back into the school, mass killing, and subsequent suicide is believed to be an impromptu, if unintended, act. At best, their plan B.

Understanding the concept of suspect advantage will help police officers realize that speed is not necessarily in the vast majority of critical incidents. Success in these events is actually increased when we do the opposite, slow down. We can't beat the suspect with speed, so we need to use better decision-making and information processing.

Slow down.

15: The Situation Dictates the Tactics

"I see what I see, but what is it supposed to be?"

In 2014, 12-year-old Tamir Rice was playing in a park near his home in Cleveland, Ohio. He was playing by himself, holding a toy gun. This has been a game played by young children, especially boys, since the invention of toy guns.

It is immortalized and watched religiously each December in the epic holiday movie, A Christmas Story [34].

Some have put the blame on Tamir Rice for his own killing, saying he shouldn't have been playing with a toy gun in public. This is abhorrent and ignorant. It is also a less than thinly veiled bigoted defense of the police officer.

The blame should rest firmly on law enforcement and the overriding attitude of fear we instill in officers and the poor decision making it produces.

Tamir was seen by a person walking through the park carrying the toy gun. This person called the police and reported what they saw. The person told the police call taker they called more just as an FYI than to report a crime.

The reporting person even told the police dispatcher that they believed it was a child playing with a toy gun. This last information was not relayed to the responding officers, a training officer and his new trainee.

Keep in mind the concepts we have talked about. Perception versus Intent, the Safety Priorities, and space and time, as I introduce the next concept; the situation dictates the tactics.

The responding officers, trained in common fear-based principles, went into this call most likely perceiving they were going to confront a man with a gun, engaged in or about to engage in a violent crime. Police can sometimes trick themselves by thinking, "Why else would the police be called if a crime wasn't being committed?"

In a 2017 Vox online news article, journalist German Lopez reported some of the post incident investigation [35]. This included the poor training performance of the trainee officer, Timothy Loehmann, when he was employed by another Ohio police agency. Loehmann's poor firearm performance was quoted in a police training report as "dismal".

It is unclear if Loehmann's poor performance was related to skills/abilities or decision making, but since his actual overall performance in a real-life incident had the observed horrible results, the specific deficiency could be considered irrelevant.

The article also recounts a US Department of Justice report resulting from a 2014 investigation into the entire Cleveland Division of Police. In this DOJ report of the Cleveland Police Department in general, the DOJ determined officer preparation, training and support deficiencies were factors that contributed to significant policing deficiencies.

In the DOJ's words:

> We found that CDP officers commit tactical errors that endanger both themselves and others in the Cleveland community and, in some instances, may result in constitutional violations.
>
> They too often fire their weapons in a manner and in circumstances that place innocent bystanders in danger; and accidentally fire them, sometimes fortuitously hitting nothing and other times shooting people and seriously injuring them.
>
> CDP officers too often use dangerous and poor tactics to try to gain control of suspects, which results in the application of additional force or places others in danger.
>
> Critically, officers do not make effective use of de-escalation techniques, too often instead escalating encounters and employing force when it may not be needed and could be avoided. While these tactical errors may not always result in constitutional violations, they place officers, suspects, and other members of the Cleveland community at risk.
>
> –Investigation of the
> Cleveland Division of Police,
> December 4, 2014[36]

This specific indictment of the Cleveland police can be justifiably applied to law enforcement in general. While specific agencies in the US do operate at high levels of performance, accountability, and public trust, we cannot deny the countless incidents of shootings, physical and verbal assaults, and illegalities committed by police prove there is a profession wide need for reform.

The concept that the situation dictates the tactics encompasses a few of our already discussed principles. We take into account the facts and information of the situation, and then consider how our preconceived perceptions may take our decision making in a certain direction. We must also work to learn or at least consider the intent of the other person in the interaction.

Understanding the situation will help us do a much better job of setting our goals toward a successful resolution. Setting realistic and accurate goals will drive our strategies in a more productive direction than if we just start snowballing through an event with no clear direction other than our self-preservation at all costs.

I often see officers in the police tactical training arena neglect to allow the situation to dictate their tactics. One display is the use of incorrect movement based on the mission.

Because of limited training time, teams condense their tactics into one or two options. They erroneously claim to use a variety of search movement speeds, and tactics. But they really use a very limited number of available resources.

Limited resources equal limited options.

Police special operations uses three main styles of movement, with some variations as the situation dictates.

1) First is covert or very slow movement. This is used to locate suspects barricaded without hostages or hiding from detection. This style is the most static, with minutes of very little physical movement and more time spent utilizing all 5 senses to detect the location of the suspect prior to direct contact or engagement.

Shields, robot cameras, and mirrors are utilized to locate suspect positions without direct engagement. The goal with this movement is to locate a suspect without a direct confrontation where the suspect has the advantage.

2) Next is a warrant service movement pace. This pace is slightly faster than covert and combines repeated verbal announcements to give a suspect the motivation to give up prior to confrontation. Announcements also serve to proclaim the authority and legal standing to be in a lo cation. The pace of movement can be described as a slow walk. Verbal commands and announcements eliminate the need to be extremely slow.

3) A third style is a deliberate hostage rescue speed, where officers are moving at a deliberate or walking pace, typically because they know where they are going to rescue hostages.

Problems happen when teams rush into a location with the same speed to apprehend a suspect as they would use to rescue a hostage. (Violation of the Safety Priorities)

If we do not consider the situation, we will use incorrect tactics or tools to solve the problem. Picture trying to drive a screw into wood using a hammer.

Looking at many of the incidents used as examples in this book or that you know of, I ask the following questions.

1) In any of these situations how did speed help the officers or teams?

2) Did the teams have surprise or was the element of surprise a factor that led to their success?

3) How can police ever use violence of action in the resolution of a critical incident unless it is a decisive action to neutralize a suspect in the effort to rescue a hostage, or stop an active assailant? Our use of force is in response to suspect actions and cannot be preemptive in most cases.

A new tactical mantra

In civilian police tactics we are governed by too many policies, procedures, laws, and ethical considerations for those tactics to benefit us except in very specific circumstances. We must always respect Constitutional rights.

Police officers can't violate someone's federal rights by "predetermining" we will be overwhelmingly violent.

Likewise, we must constantly evaluate and update our evaluation. If they are not a threat, or stop being a threat we cannot just go HAM on suspects. Police officers can't use unrestrained speed in any incident.

One question I ask students is, "How fast do you want to run into a gunfight?" Not an active shooter event or a hostage rescue, but a straight up gunfight. Suspect versus police.

Any time bullets fly, we run the potential of being shot. We would be in violation of the Safety Priorities by putting confronting the suspect above officer safety.

When we violate tactical principles, we increase the potential for tragedy.

I believe we should replace this antiquated and obsolete mantra of "speed, surprise, and violence of action" with a new one. I suggest the following:

> "Mission-based movement, tactical dilemmas, and appropriate action"

Mission-based movement is a better reminder for officers of what we expect of ourselves. Words matter. When using the old mantra officers will move faster than they can accurately think. The gauge for your pace or speed isn't "move as fast as you can accurately shoot."

The real gauge for movement pace is to move only as fast as you can accurately process information.

LEOs who rush into situations overwhelm their ability to think and process information accurately. Because of the OODA Loop processing delay, we will almost always be the recipient of violent action before we can respond.

Or worse, we will predetermine the need to shoot since we don't want to lose the OODA loop battle and, denying ourselves time to process the reality, will shoot the 10-year-old child holding a cell phone hiding in the bedroom.

If we instill and train the mentality that officers use the correct movement for the mission they are involved in, they will proceed cautiously when appropriate and move quickly when the situation dictates it.

Tactical dilemmas are created using tactical options, contingencies, and a variety of resources and tools. Had the Florida deputies who shot Dylan Scott used space and time, less lethal tools, and organized team tactics, they would have created a dilemma for the suspect.

He could sit in the car, possibly get bitten by a K9, struck with a baton round, contaminated by chemical agent, or give up. His dilemma would be that he would not have been able to succeed in his original plan to force the deputy to shoot him.

They would have taken the advantage away from the suspect, subverted his plan to make them shoot him and, more probably, been able to arrest him using decisive less lethal force, or perhaps no force at all. Scott's plan would have been useless, and without a plan B, surrender would be the only other option.

One of my team leaders, Lt. Dan Murphy, a person for whom I would go to Hell and arrest the Devil, and one of my best friends, coined the term "trifecta". This is the use of at least three tactical options, sequentially, to create an overwhelming dilemma for a suspect that results in a psychological and, possibly, physiological shut down.

We used this tactic in the arrests of many high-risk suspects and suicidal subjects.

Combined options might include the use of a distraction device, a chemical agent, and an impact munition. Maybe a K9, if appropriate. But at least three different stimulus producing tools, one after the other in fairly quick succession.

We once performed a “rescue” on a sex assault probation violation suspect who barricaded himself in a truck, armed with a shotgun, and claimed to be “suicidal”. A patrol officer/SWAT operator located him and, after conducting a traffic stop, noticed the suspect had a shotgun. So began a vehicle barricade and SWAT call out.

Though he claimed to be suicidal, he was primarily a wanted fugitive. We considered all of these factors and devised a plan where we would use several tools and tactics to create a tactical dilemma for him, to motivate him to surrender. We picked a moment in which he wasn't ready to shoot to initiate our plan.

While he was speaking to a negotiator by phone and wiping tears from his eyes (can't shoot a shotgun with no hands), we broke his rear window with a kinetic baton round, launched chemical agents into his truck, and deployed a distraction device in front of his truck. This caused the suspect to panic, politely set the phone on the ground next to the truck and drive away. Kind of.

> (Seriously. He took the time to not damage our phone. Would a truly suicidal person be concerned that he might get charged with criminal mischief if he ruined a police agency's throw phone while being arrested?)

He tried to drive away, but the powder (intentional) chemical agent just swirled around the truck cab, affecting him even more. It also obscured his vision. He stopped the truck. As a preplanned action, we jumped in our vehicles and followed.

He stopped after about 100 feet. We stopped and continued to strike him with Pepper balls and Sage Ordnance 37mm rubber baton rounds. The suspect opened his door, with his arm extended outward holding the door.

The K9, also preplanned, launched and latched on the suspect's arm, playing tug of war with the suspect. The suspect was motivated to get out of the vehicle and lie down prone on the ground per our commands. Actually, he didn't hear anything we were saying. He was in pain.

We slowly approached him, with less lethal and lethal options, and while giving continuous commands for him to comply, safely took him into custody.

The shotgun he had was stolen and contained three rounds. Not at all coincidentally, we were alerted to him by his ex-girlfriend who told us he was trying to find her, her mother, and her daughter. 3 rounds, 3 people.

So, as we think about the sincerity of his suicidal claims, we may wonder why he would load a shogun with three shells, when one would definitely do the job. Or, if he was considering suicide by cop, why would he not want to hurt our phone or upset us with his actions?

Most criminal suspects are not suicidal, nor do they have a death wish.

We developed a plan, with several contingencies, and as the suspect responded to our actions, we employed more planned tactics. And we combined them to create the dilemma that eventually caused him to want to get away from his truck and surrender.

He surrendered even knowing he was likely to go to prison for at least 25 years, as a sex offender. Being a sex offender in prison is very difficult, since upstanding, honorable, proper criminals all look down on sex offenders.

This is what effective principle-based decision making combined with proven tactics does for civilian law enforcement.

We can enter into a chaotic, unpredictable critical incident, and using solid principles and tactics, control the environment and direct the other people involved in the event into a more predictable path, slowing the pace of the situation to a point where we can effectively stop the runaway train safely and under control.

Scenario training during a SWAT course.

16: Scenario-Based Training

"No ninjas out of the ceiling."

More and more agencies are going to simulation trainers, computer/projector combinations with interactive videos. Special weapons with lasers, virtual reality goggles, and computer programs can provide a variety of scenarios. While these are better than nothing, I am not a fan of too much technology for police training.

These simulators only have so many different scenarios and a certain number of variations of those scenarios. Plus, the dialog is set. It cannot be tweaked mid scenario.

Police officers are expert cheats when it comes to training. Nobody wants to "fail in training" and look bad, so officers memorize these simulation scenarios and position themselves where they won't get shot by the suspect who hasn't even shown themselves yet.

Officers learn where to stand so the sensors don't "see" them. VR counters that but is still limited on scenario variations. I still believe real life role players provide the best prompts and reactions in scenario-based training.

Scenario Based Training, SBT, is the best way to train officers and improve their critical thinking and decision-making abilities alongside their practical skills. Just as using Simunition marking cartridge force-on-force weapons is the closest we can replicate real life shooting situations, SBT is the closest officers can come to real incidents.

The great thing about SBT is the "real world" interaction in a totally safe environment. Absent lax or derelict training safety protocol, participants will never be in actual jeopardy. Even though the environment is safe, the participants still experience the physical, emotional, and psychological effects of being in real incidents. The mind and body work together but are also detached.

Athletes have long used creative visualization to improve their performances. They can think about performing and their mind will trick their body into thinking it is actually performing, even while standing still or otherwise motionless. Watch diving athletes before they make a dive.

Scenario training works the same way. Even though the participant cannot really be shot or injured, the fear and worry they would feel in a real event is still experienced. The scenarios can be stopped restarted, adjusted, increased or decreased in complexity, to help officers overcome those fears and worries.

SBT is better than the computer simulators because if the trainer identifies a very specific deficiency, they can alter a scenario in tiny ways to help an officer overcome the deficiency.

Start Slow

SBT allows trainers to start slow and build up to very complex problems with many moving parts. We can also design a scenario to address a specific concept like space and time.

And we can adjust the threat to be something that "sends a message" or is more impactful. This might be the difference between a suspect aggressively engaging the officer or merely walking out of a doorway, if the officer gets too close too quickly. Unless this action has been recorded and is programmed into the computer, it can't be produced on the spot.

High tech versus *Now* tech.

If we have new officers with little experience, we can do "crawl, walk, run" with them. Role players can be cooperative, and as officers gain confidence just speaking to people, we can add subtle changes. A role player moves too close while talking. A suspect keeps putting their hands in their pockets. Does the officer address these concerns, or not even notice?

Scenarios can be developed to become incrementally more complex. This allows the participants to move through their OODA loops with an appropriate amount of stress, while still giving them the ability to think.

Keep Stress Low

Training should not be high stress all the time. Sometimes, trainers feel they need to prove something to officers. This is all ego. As a trainer it's not about me showing how cool I am, how much I know, or how good I am at creating no-win situations. This is the sign of a poor trainer.

A trainer's job is to provide a positive learning environment. Too many trainers want to create a false picture of a horrific world where the boogey man lurks around every corner and "you will get killed!" Fear, fear, fear.

Dr. Maxwell Maltz talks about stress and its relationship to learning in his book Psycho-Cybernetics [37], originally written in the early 1960's. Maltz said, "The more intense the crisis situation under which you learn, the less you learn."

In actual practice, overstimulation will cause a person to reduce down their thoughts, options, and thinking to very limited responses. If they haven't ingrained it, they won't access it. The student will not develop new thoughts, ideas, or create, when they are highly stressed. Their thinking will collapse down to very basic survival actions.

We don't rise to the level of the occasion. We sink to the level of our training.

We see this in officers with little experience, or who have only been subjected to high stress training. They instantly go to survival, usually overreacting by shooting the role player in an obvious no shoot situation. More fear. Where have we seen this "shoot first" scenario play out in real life?

This doesn't mean officers should not experience any stress in training. They should and will experience stress. Depending on their experience and confidence, merely searching an empty building will produce enough stress to fog their safety goggles or protective helmet.

There is a difference between training to teach and training to evaluate.

Evaluation training is where more stress will be injected into the scenario. A good trainer understands that to induce stress you don't need to have a role player in a Red Man suit do a full-frontal attack every scenario.

By reducing the stress in teaching scenarios, officers can better reason through their response. They can build confidence and reduce their primordial fear.

As officers process information, they will make the connection between principles and tactics, understanding how to apply them in the correct way and at the correct time. They will understand how to stack contingencies in their mind and access relevant tools and tactics to fit the need in that moment.

Operate in this moment but plan for the next.

One of my repetitive mantras is "what now? What next?" I ask this as students are moving through a scenario if they appear to "lock up", stop working, or seem like they think they are done. The world doesn't stop on the shot, our training shouldn't either.

By this I mean, many police agencies, and especially tactical teams, run a scenario up to the act of shooting. The officers engage the suspect, “put them down”, then break character, end scenario, whatever you call it, and talk about where they hit with their shots. Or where they think they hit with their shots.

I see it training SWAT operators. They will shoot, then just stop. When I tell them to keep working the problem, they don’t know what to do. They have a hard time completing a radio transmission. They don’t do self-checks to see if they’ve been hit. They don't think about "What's next."

Again, we don’t rise to the level of the occasion. We sink to the level of our training.

Our scenario training should include all actions we want our officers to take during any crisis response. If it is an arrest, they should work through to custody (without real handcuffing, ouch!) and preparation for transport.

If a shooting scenario, they should work through to being relieved and removed from the scene. And they should practice all the considerations that come with securing the scene. If not in physical movement, they should talk through their plan.

My SWAT team used to practice to the point of questioning operators why they shot during the scenario. What did they see that they determined required lethal force. We started this practice after 3 of our team members were involved in an Officer Involved Shooting (OIS).

We realized our live fire shooting training didn't involve explaining our actions. You can't justify shooting the target because you know it's a "shoot" target. If we shoot at threats (what we know), when it really counts (in court), how do we explain why we shot. In an effort to develop our confidence, competence, professionalism, and knowledge, we realized we needed to practice explaining our actions.

Law enforcement officers must always be able to explain their actions.

By doing this we improve our ability to process information faster. If we know we need to be sure of what we are doing, we get better at processing. We get faster at progressing through options. If we can't shoot, we quickly plan our next best course of action. It also helps with noticing details.

The devil is in the details.

Our brains work like computers. A computer program must be loaded for a computer to run the appropriate functions.

In the old days, computers used punch cards to perform functions. If the punch card was punched wrong, the computer would not perform the task correctly. If it was punched correctly, success. But only for that specific task.

We want our brains to work like AI, Artificial Intelligence. It may be better called Critical Intelligence, CI. We want to ensure officers are learning, creating, building on all the information they take in.

Scenario based training allows officers to develop their CI, rather than be punch card processors that have very limited ability to contingency plan and adapt to changing situations. Officers will see options other than to "just shoot" because they haven't simply been "punch carded" by poor training to do so.

In case you missed it, **we won't rise to the level of the occasion. We will sink to the level of our training.**

17: Teaching to Your Audience

"We are all adults here"

As trainers, we want to instill good tactics and decision-making skills, while impressing the importance of all the relevant topics like situational awareness, officer safety, or solid arrest control and defensive tactics skills. Sending young inexperienced officers, and even salty veterans, out into the dangerous world can cause some anxiety in the old "sensei".

We worry whether or not we told officers everything they need to know to be safe and do their job well. Police training runs a fine line between being too soft or easy for officers and being a military bootcamp. Several years ago, I taught a SWAT Basic class in Tennessee. On the first morning, new SWAT operators filed into the room.

As new instructors, we usually try to break the ice by saying hello, welcome and easing our way into the heart of the material. We try to tell some stories to lighten things up and set the tone for the week. Again, I try to lower the stress when possible. We got through the first hour of introductions, administrative issues, and logistics.

We took a break and two guys in the row of desks and chairs breathed a sigh of relief and slumped in their seats. (the class was one long row across the room, not multiple rows) One of them, a friend of mine to this day, said,

"Man, we were just waiting for you to start flipping over desks, screaming at everyone, and telling us to get outside to PT (Physical training). We went to another SWAT class and that's what they did."

I teach the material I am discussing in this book, only intensified and multiplied. Our courses are heavy on learning, developing critical thinking and decision-making skills, along with the physical tactics. Our practical portion is meant to get operators a lot of physical repetition of the tactics. We don't waste time running around, singing songs.

It is my sincere belief that police trainers who want to "smoke" their students with physical exercise don't have anything to teach. Why else would you devote precious training time to running or lifting heavy things?

I am there to help you improve your service to your community, your personal safety, and your benefit to your agency. In that order. I'm not there to bring you a cool new kettlebell workout, or some new CrossFit WOD. That stuff is done on the operators' own time. Do you even CrossFit, bro?

Read the Room

Those two in the class are very competent officers, operating well above the level of an average officer. But they were so anxious during that entire hour, waiting for some chaos to jump off, I am not sure what, if anything, they heard us say.

If we create an anxiety ridden training environment, especially in a lecture or classroom setting, the very people who need the information most won't get it because they are mentally preparing to do some over-their-head hardcore PT stuff.

Civilian police are not military special forces soldiers. We can lament this fact all we want; they still won't be SF soldiers. Because they are not soldiers. They are civilian police. And outside of the special weapons and tactics community, the majority of LEOs don't want to do high speed stuff. Most just want to do the minimum and are happy to be unexceptional.

Police officers are all adults of varying skills, abilities, interests, and motivation.

Work to create a positive training environment. The goal is to get them to learn. If you come off like a Marine Corp Boot Camp Drill Instructor, you will lose most of your audience, and your job as a trainer. When I teach, I give much positive feedback and encouragement. I learned to do this when I coached my son's 8th grade football team.

During our summer practices, our offense was working, and I was watching my different quarterbacks. We ran a play, and the QB looked like he went through his progressions, then heaved the ball down field to a receiver running flat out. The receiver didn't catch the ball. The ball was there, the receiver just didn't catch it.

Everyone turned, I mean everyone, and looked at me. It was dead quiet. I asked the 13-year-old kid why he threw the ball deep. He locked up. I repeated my question three more times. Each time he just stood quiet.

The other QB said, "Coach, he's scared. Last year, every time he made any mistake the coach would yell and scream at him."

I called a stop to practice, had the entire team come up to me and I told them, "Everyone, this year is not last year. I don't know how the other coach did things, but I do things different.

You are 8th graders playing a game. The goal is to have fun the great game of football. I will not yell and scream at you, and I expect the same maturity out of you."

Then I looked at the kid and asked again, "Why did you throw the ball deep?"

He said, "I saw he was open."

"Perfect. Excellent decision."

I turned to the receiver and said, "Now catch the ball."

We had a great year! All of the boys played, contributed, and learned how much fun football is to play.

If you're training officers and they are too intimidated, too angry, or too checked out because of how you interact, they are not learning anything. I get it. Police work is dangerous, and you must prepare them for the violent world outside the wire. Remember…

Police officers are 5-10 times less likely than the public to be killed in police/public interactions.

Maybe we should train the public for the dangerous world of police interaction.

Be positive.

Failure does not breed success unless it comes with lessons on how to be successful after the experience of not succeeding. I don't even like to use the word failure. I call such events learning experiences.

Failure can't happen in training. It can only happen in the real world. And even then, it is only a failure if you don't try again.

We need to stop injecting fear and negativity just to show how cool we are as a trainer. We need to stop creating no-win scenarios where officers get "killed" in order to show "how dangerous the job is" and that "maybe they don't belong."

A fellow instructor once told me of an event during a SWAT basic school on the east coast. There was a female operator going through the course. A role player from the host agency felt he needed to show this "little girl" how the SWAT world is for "big boys".

In a scenario, the role player grabbed her. In violation of safety protocol, she hadn't removed her "back up" butterfly knife from her vest prior to training. And nobody else knew she kept a knife there. She produced the knife, and almost stabbed the role player. Great response to the stimulus. I think she belongs.

We can't rise to the level of the occasion. We can only sink to the level of our training.

Since training is the place where we want learning to occur, we should create and operate an environment that has the maximum potential to encourage the most learning possible. Otherwise, we are wasting everyone's time.

For many officers, training day is a time of stress because they don't feel confident about their skills and tactics. They think they are the only one in the agency who can't do the technique. They may be out of shape, older, or not the silent ninja assassin officer who learns naturally, has great technique, and always seems so comfortable.

We were conducting our agency's yearly training one summer. A team of officers was moving down a hall and a role player was standing in a little cubby hole. The "suspect" was not trying to hide other than standing still in a narrow space.

An older officer, who fit my above description, but NOT the silent ninja part, didn't see the suspect, though he easily should have. The role player suspect shot at the team. We stopped; everyone was looking at the officer who "got the team shot". He needed to save face.

He complained about the force-on-force helmet, in this case a Simunition brand fx-9000 I think was the model. It had an elastic band inside it that was supposed to go around the back of the wearer's head. In his case, because he didn't pay attention when we were giving instructions to make sure that band was out of the way, it had fallen down in front of his eyes. He blinded himself.

The other officers were kind of laughing at him. He was normally a total practical joker and comedian. Not today. He was embarrassed, bad. I saw myself at a crossroads. I could laugh at him too or do something else. I had been training nationally for about 4 years at that point.

In front of everyone I said, "Don't even trip. This happens all the time. You know I teach all over the country. For some reason this band tends to work its way over your head and in front of your face. I see it a lot."

He immediately relaxed. I explained a "trick" to getting it to stay back and helped him put on the helmet. He shook his head a couple of times and said he thought it was much better. Until he retired a few years later, every training we had, he was involved and actively participated. And he was more relaxed in the trainings.

I have never in my career seen that band go from the back to the front. I had never seen the band blind anyone before him. And the "trick" was to hold the strap in back as you put on the helmet. Amazing!

What I did was make him not seem like such a dope. And since I trained all over the country, I had credibility and standing to say if it was just him or a problem with the helmet. Consider if I made him out to be the problem. I could have screwed up the entire group.

He would be mad because I made fun of him. Other officers who liked him would be mad at me for doing that. Younger officers would see that dynamic and not want to be the butt of any jokes or be made fun of either. Now, everyone is either mad or afraid to do anything that gets them ridiculed. Training is over, thank you for your participation.

I know some of you are right now thinking about trainers you had who created a negative environment just like this. Some of you are that trainer. The great thing is you now have some new ideas and ways to change from a negative encouragement trainer to a positive one. Trust me, your students will be happier, and so will you.

The training environment is filled with diverse learners. Some learn by hearing, some by seeing, some by doing. Most through some combination of the three. But in the police world, we are all adults and should be treated like adults.

Understand what motivates your students to work and to not work. Keep the training moving along, fun, and challenging. Keep the vibe positive and use encouragement instead of ridicule. The goal is for the students to listen to, learn, and then use the amazing information you are dispensing.

18: Training Happens Everywhere

"Tabletops. Not Just for Dancing Anymore"

The Training "Spectrum" What passes for training in US police departments is as varied as the uniforms and badges the different agencies wear. I have taught from the smallest agencies, a one officer agency in Northern North Dakota, to the largest, NYPD. You might be surprised at how close those two extremes are in regard to frequency of training.

There is no national standard of training. No common level of performance extends across the spectrum. I will use police special weapons to illustrate how varied training and training time can be, across the policing spectrum.

According to established best practices from top trainers and national organizations, SWAT teams are supposed to conduct at least two 8-hour training days per month, plus a yearly 40-hour team school. This amounts to only 232 hours per year to maintain proficiency in over a dozen special weapons and tactics skills and proficiencies. Now consider the east coast model of ESU (Emergency Services Unit) rather than SWAT or ERT (Emergency Response Team).

An ESU team is tasked with traditional police SWAT duties, plus a number of special response duties normally performed by the Fire Department. They perform automobile accident extrications, building high-angle rescues, and water/ice rescues. Maybe you can figure out how a high level of proficiency can be maintained in so many disciplines, because I can't.

Most ESU teams are part time. The officers must also work their normal job hours too. Something will atrophy and, in my experience, what falls away is principle-based decision making and tactical options training.

If a tactical team, more highly motivated, skilled, and trained than the average line officer, is only receiving that amount of training and proficiency, think of how little tactical decision-making training the majority of US police agencies provide to the average line officer.

Training is What You Make it

I was in an east coast state training a group of instructors. We were at a large empty commercial building that allowed police agencies to train in it until it got resold and repurposed.

When we arrived for the class, a local SWAT team was already in the lot preparing the conduct their training day. I always like to see how other teams train, so I paid attention to their tempo. Remember, they were all there before we started our training at 8am.

Around 9:30am, they all walked into the building together, finally geared up (wearing their ballistic gear with their weapons) to start training. We were teaching and running scenarios, the students were conducting scenarios, and we were moving inside and outside the building.

Around 11:30am, we watched a pizza delivery show up and unload a bunch of pizzas. By the time we broke for lunch, at 12:00pm, the local team was well into their pizza lunch.

At 1:10pm, when we started back up working scenarios and teaching again, the local team was still enjoying their pizza break. They put their gear back on and managed to get back inside for more training at about 2:00pm.

At 3:45pm, we were outside working on a scenario where officers move from the parking lot into the building as a team. The local team began trickling out of the front doors, in between our groups entering. They were obviously done training for the day.

One of the students in the class came over to me and reminded me of something I had talked about earlier in the week that "training occurs in a spectrum". It has a wide range of appearances. He said, "You were right. I bet they call what they did today a full training day. But I haven't seen them do much of it."

At 5:15 pm when we drove out of the lot, about half of the local team was still standing around leaning on their vehicles talking about their great training day, or whatever. Giving them the benefit that as soon as they entered the building, they were training, I figured they actually worked about 4 hours out of their 8-hour day.

To me, that is robbery. You just stole 4 hours of time from your community. Not your agency, your community. You don't work for your agency. You work for the people you protect.

They are paying you do be ready to do a tough, possibly dangerous job on their behalf. Since you cannot plan for when that job might happen, you need to be prepared all the time.

We will never rise to the level of the occasion. We will only ever sink to the level of our training.

Training doesn't need a Broadway Producer and Director

Often when I talk to officers about setting aside training time, the big excuse is "we try but it hard getting everyone together." That's the problem. You will never get everyone together, unless you are the one officer agency. And even then, you are probably of two minds about every decision, including lunch.

Then there is the top heavy 14-agency, multiple discipline response training that includes 130 people, role players with moulage injuries (you know, the movie makeup), bombs, kids screaming and running, and all that nonsense. We did that once or twice. It was really more a waste of time.

We did a multi-agency active shooter response training once with three other teams, two fire departments, and dozens of other people. Our team's role was to go after the suspects, with two other teams.

The organizers didn't get enough suspects for each team to search for suspects; we were all looking for the same 2 suspects. 2 minutes into the whole scenario another team found and shot both. So, we pretended to search for a bit, eventually getting done after about 45 minutes.

The entire scenario lasted 4 hours, most of it with us standing around, trying to train while not get in anyone else's way. Not the most productive. Plus, the after action debrief was held in the parking lot. Couldn't hear much. At all. I hope somebody got something out of it.

I have found that we cannot replicate the true chaos of a real event. We can train our decision making and tactics, making them second nature, so in a real event, we can perform almost on auto pilot, and have more RAM available to handle the varied emotional aspects.

If we need to think too much about the mechanics, we will lock up trying to deal with our humanity colliding with the overwhelming horror of the event.

Our major scenario went way too long, and we did way too little in it. The organizers could have created a complete scenario for each SWAT team, but that would have necessitated many more role players, monitors, and logistical considerations. Bigger, bigger, bigger.

I have found the best way to prepare, and train is repetition, with time to evaluate, adjust, and reinforce. The scale should be small, so it can be repeated often. It's all about the "reps".

Think small and Fast

When I teach, I run short scenarios, at most 5 minutes long, and usually about 2-3 minutes. This gives me the ability to watch and remember actions or decisions for critique. Plus, if officers are exhibiting bad habits, running long scenarios gives them the ability to solidify those bad habits before you can correct them.

I don't like to interrupt the scenario for correction, unless it is really bad, or creates an officer safety or scenario safety issue. By officer safety I mean just really poor tactics, and scenario safety means it is unsafe in real time and someone might get injured for real, for real.

When developing and conducting scenarios, we should determine whether they are to teach or to evaluate. If teaching, we may correct as we go. If evaluating, we should let the officers "mess up", get shot with marking rounds, or miss a suspect. Correction will come after. But we must know that we cannot evaluate something if we haven't taught it.

A poor instructor will run officers through a frustrating scenario without any prior teaching, then criticize (not critique) their actions, as though the students should have known how to do it. Nobody learns in that environment. Scenarios can be very short if they are focused on a very specific teaching point.

If I want to teach about space and time, I will create a scenario specific for this concept. I may set up the scenario of the Florida deputies with the potentially armed suspect in a vehicle. I will run the scenario just like the real event, and maybe have the "suspect" exit the vehicle quickly. I will watch the officers' actions and decision making. Then stop.

I will reset the suspect in the car, restart the scenario, then move the officers back about 10 feet to a position of cover. I will then have the suspect exit the vehicle again. Then stop.

I ask the officers about how they felt each time. In which position did they feel they could process information better? Which position just felt better?

I can run both scenarios, with critiques and changes, in about 3-4 minutes. What I want is for the officers to see and feel both experiences.

Feeling discomfort in training is much more manageable than feeling it in real life. The feeling of discomfort in a real event is what causes the snowball effect where officers gain uncontrollable momentum, usually resulting in several regrettable decisions and at least one major tragedy.

Tabletop Scenarios and Discussions

Tabletop discussions can be very helpful for training. As we talked about before, your mind and body can't differentiate if you are actually performing an action or merely thinking about performing it. You can talk about a response to an incident and for your mind it will be as though you have physically done it.

This kind of training is great for small groups, like shifts before going in-service. Pick some real event and talk about how you as a shift, as an agency, would handle it. This does a few really good things.

1) It gets everyone on the same page. Each police agency has its own established policies, procedures, and accepted practices. Some agencies require their officers to carry certain tools, others make them optional.

2) Tabletop discussions of critical events help all officers, especially new or less experienced officers, understand what will most likely happen and to be ready for it. This reduces the potential that an inexperienced officer will shoot their firearm sympathetically because they heard another officer deploy a taser.

   It provides quick and easy training in a relaxed atmosphere where performance anxiety won't inhibit officers from "taking chances". It is much easier to make a mistake in thought sitting around a table with your close coworkers than to do it in an agency wide training in front of "THE INSTRUCTORS".

3) With the unpredictable nature of policing, what you discuss as a hypothetical in shift briefing may happen in real life 10 minutes later. How nice would it be have already run a successful rehearsal of your resolution?

   Of course, the real event has the variable of a different subject/suspect, but having laid the foundation, you are in a better place to deal with that variable and have your contingencies already pre thought out.

Formal, consistent, and ongoing agency level training is often left to dissolve because it becomes too cumbersome and too much effort to conduct. Training is seen as this "big deal" that "somebody has to put together". We can increase our training time by thinking in smaller time increments.

When I experienced my first college football practice, I was shocked. We did some drills for 3 minutes, others for 7 minutes. Seriously. The first time my coach said. "Ok. We got 3 minutes of taking on the tight ends.", I thought, "how can we do anything in 3 minutes?"

Well, it's called efficiency. We were just trying to get a couple reps, build some muscle memory, and then we were on to the next phase of practice.

When I was a day camp counselor our boss would remind us to stop the game when the kids were having the most fun. Don't keep playing until they get tired and bored. If you stop at the height of fun, the kids will remember it as positive, and want to play it again. They will also be more likely to engage in the next thing you do, since their interest, excitement, and desire to participate is high.

Keep the stress low, and keep people engaged through questions, compliments, encouragement, and participation. Avoid negative environments and constant criticizing. Don't nitpick. We are not developing Spartan Warriors. (NO, we are not.) We are trying to give our officers simple and effective physical, mental, and emotional tools to help them do a successful job serving the public, eventually retiring intact, after a long and rewarding career.

A holistic approach to supporting the police.

19: Support for Officer Training

"No Man is an Island"

Administrative and Organizational Support

The previous preparation and training concepts and principles will improve officers' confidence, abilities, and investment in their job. They will also help facilitate the restoration of public trust and the improvement of the public/police relationship.

All of these mindset and training improvements can be done from the individual officer level, up to the entire profession. These principles and concepts do not need any formal programs, edicts, or endorsements to be implemented and developed. But, in order for them to be sustainable, there must be organizational backing and support.

Agency administrators must see this effort to return to comprehensive community policing as equal, or greater, in importance to data driven policing. Everything I have talked about is intended to be done within the parameters of a community-oriented policing/public safety model.

This is human-centered policing, done by interacting with others on a human level first. If we only see our interactions as numbers on a data sheet, to be quantified not qualified, we will remain where we are presently, lacking wholesale public support and trust.

As I said in an earlier chapter, the numbers don't lie, but they also don't cry. We need to get past the antiseptic presentation of data to diffuse or dismiss human involved and emotion-laden events.

We can't continue to respond to families with cold data and apathetic rhetoric like "police must make split second decisions in a rapidly changing environment" when they question why their family member suffering a mental health break was shot and killed by police.

Or why their autistic son was injected with a lethal dose of tranquilizer while trying to return home from the store.

This dismissal does nothing to help a person grieve or understand the decision made by law enforcement that took the life of their family member. Police administrators must look at these situations from a new perspective and ask themselves some questions.

1) Did we use human-centered decision making in this situation, based on the Safety Priorities, Dual life value theory, situation dictates tactics, our tools, tactics and training, etc.?

2) If we didn't, or don't use these foundational principles, could using them have made a positive difference

3) Are we using all available tools and resources to solve problems or are we using contrived rhetoric to explain away our incompetence and lack of desire to improve our service?

4) If this was our family member, would we be satisfied with our explanation? Would we be ok that the police just shot our 91-year-old blind and deaf grandma? Or our 52-year-old brother/pastor having a psychotic break?

If we cannot answer yes, or we refuse to ask these honest and introspective questions, we need to change how we see the world, our jobs, and how we see our role and responsibility to the community.

We need to admit we don't really care about the people who are paying us to care about them.

If we cannot answer these questions, but would like to answer "yes", we should make the decision to improve our training and our commitment to our officers and, subsequently, our community.

They are paying us to care about them enough to solve tough problems, not kill them one at a time.

Invest in Police-relevant Training.

Once administrators realize the need for improvement, the first step should be to allocate and invest in quality outside training. Good knowledge and tactics need to be installed prior to a critical incident. Officers won't improve in the moment. We solve problems before they are ever encountered. You solve the problem through adequate and relevant training. For police that means police relevant or police specific training.

The combination of a plethora of former military operators looking for employment and the belief that military training is somehow better than police training has spawned a whole new arena of trainers providing military tactics training to civilian police. This has had some undesired affects.

Soldiers do not work within the US federal, state, and municipal legal system. They do not have LE policies and procedures in mind.

I have talked to and watched military trainers teach police. I have attended their trainings. When asked about certain concerns and requirements police have based on their specific environments, these trainers are void of the answers needed by police officers.

They also operate under the premise of an acceptable casualty rate for any operation. In policing no casualties are acceptable. This is the basis of the Safety Priorities; step one in the 5-Step Process.

If a subject/suspect must be injured or neutralized in a situation, it should be because all other means have either proved or would prove ineffective in curbing the person's dangerous actions.

Our decision to use force, especially lethal force, should be a well-reasoned decision, not merely because we got surprised (Tamir Rice, Atatiana Jefferson) or because we were scared of a possible fist fight (Patrick Warren Sr., Andre Hill).

Police administrators must ensure their tactical teams subscribe to current civilian police best practices in the police tactical community. They should discourage their teams from adopting all the military SPECOPS mentality, gear, and trappings that do not support a civilian law enforcement paradigm. Now everybody thinks they need NVG or Night Vision Goggles, capabilities.

While I agree the ability to operate in no light could be a great help in at nighttime in a densely wooded area, I question its degree of relevance in an urban environment.

I am not saying it is bad or wrong. I am saying the amount of training time that must be devoted to becoming proficient at the use of equipment like NVGs, for most teams, could be better spent somewhere else.

In my 15 years on a SWAT team and over 500 warrant services, building searches, and building entries, I know of zero times where darkness gave us an advantage to the point of wishing we had NVGs.

One decision-making principle and one industrial invention negate the need for night vision. The suspect always has tactical advantage, and the electric light bulb.

Even in the dark, the suspect is in a position we can't determine ahead of time. NVGs don't see through solid objects. A suspect hiding behind a wall, cabinet, or panel is still unseen. But they know where we are.

I have found, and we can verify this with role players, that turning on a light has a significant psychological effect on a suspect, making them feel exposed and not wanting to make a sound, let alone move.

Most suspects won't know if we are wearing NVGs, but they know we can see them if they move when we turn on lights. But SWAT teams think to be successful we need this equipment and the military entry tactic of domination.

Military room entries consist of dynamic entry followed by threat elimination (shooting, killing). Often, entry is preceded by a fragmentation grenade. Military training often neglects the most important police task in critical incidents: suspect contact and custody.

Police room entries typically require suspect location, identification, then custody. And we don't have grenades, at least not in this respect. Once the military mindset gets ingrained, it is difficult to change.

I was teaching a Basic SWAT course in Illinois. One of the students, a solid thinking person who did great work all week, was part of a group making an entry in a scenario. He was going to deploy a distraction device. As he moved up, made motion to deploy the device, he yelled, "Frag out!"

He immediately stopped himself, and said, "Wow! Did I just say that? Man, muscle memory, hunh?"

Without conducting a whole class, we do not deploy a distraction device with the same intent a soldier deploys a fragmentation grenade. It requires a different mindset and effort. And it definitely has a different result.

Administrators must realize how ingrained the military mindset might be, and where in police operations it can create counterproductive thinking and incorrect decision making.

There are plenty of high-quality police trainers who can provide excellent and professional training to officers in basic and advanced police tactics, without resorting to bringing in military trainers. Different missions require different decisions and tactics. You wouldn't fix a bicycle with a hammer and chisel. Likewise, you wouldn't sculpt a marble statue with a crescent wrench and Philips head screwdriver.

Making Time for What's Important

In this day of "more training equals better training" police administrators must understand this is a misnomer. The two don't equate. Police are trained in dozens of disciplines and specialties, including autism recognition, Narcan delivery, MH response, victim interaction, as well as all the typical police actions.

This has given officers just enough understanding to realize they know nothing. Because they are more easily overwhelmed and anxious, we are seeing our officers fail, sometimes miserably, in many areas, sometimes in the same event. What if we used a new model of policing, with two major changes?

First, we incorporate Subject Matter Experts (SME) into police response to relevant situations. MH counselors and other professionals respond to police calls alongside officers. Officers maintain situational safety and security while the professional interacts with the patient/subject.

We wouldn't need to provide officers the "CYA" couple of hours of training that does nothing but make officers more anxious. They would learn in real time, from the actual SME. Agencies, including my former agency, are incorporating this practice of combining specialists on relevant calls.

I have seen an attempt to replace police with counselors on certain calls. This is dumb and only sets everyone up for failure. When I see this, I wonder if the people who created this situation are profoundly ignorant, or intentionally working to sabotage the efforts to change the public safety model.

Effective public safety should be a collaborative effort, not a proprietary situation.

Second, give your officers adequate time to train in relevant subjects. Rather than spend 2-4 hours learning about autism, have officers train in scenario-based response to situations as police officers.

Have officers focus on the principles discussed in this book, basing their interactions on the premise they are working with people who are merely different than them, not having less human value and not "bad".

Give your officers the opportunity to develop their confidence, not just reinforce their fear, anxiety, and incompetence. Speaking of fear, don't do like an agency I know of, that tried to reduce officer training because the administration was scared to train.

The administration at my old agency tried to reduce firearms shooting and decision-making training hours simply because they didn't want to go to training. They were intimidated at training because even brand-new officers shot better and made better no-shoot decisions than them.

Instead of getting better through training, their solution was to not have the training. If we didn't have it, they couldn't look bad doing it wrong. But what about the 1-year officer who must make those decisions on a daily basis, sometimes alone in a dark alley, in the middle of the night?

Not much concern for them, it seemed. We presented the amazingly simple idea of changing the firearms training from mandatory to optional for anyone above the rank of Lieutenant. Our administrators accepted this tiny little change and training continued as it always had.

Always determine the goal (train officers) and then strategize the best route to your goal (don't argue with or call out your administration).

Consider the detrimental impact of reduction of critical skills training for new, inexperience officers, especially if you note the average experience in years of the officers getting into questionable use of force incidents around the nation. The majority seems to be well under 10 years.

We have young people with little diverse life experience getting into policing and being trained in the fear-based mindset, then not being given adequate principle-based use of force decision-making training. If people in police administration cannot see we are cooking up a recipe for disaster here, they should not be in the "big picture" positions.

I noticed throughout my career, and as I work with agencies around the country, there is a lack of personal accountability at the administrative level. In my opinion, administrative accountability shouldn't be something that has to be told exists. It should be obviously evident, almost even just "felt".

Sure, chiefs sometimes resign after high profile incidents like officers killing innocent people, or shoddy agency-wide responses to public disorder, but what about the everyday accountability?

If the head of an agency wants the credit for pioneering exceptional policing or whatever the buzz phrase du jour may be, shouldn't they also accept all the responsibility for anything that goes wrong?

No matter how small the transgression, I believe the chief, sheriff, director, etc., must readily acknowledge it is they who are ultimately responsible for any shortcomings of their officers.

If the head of an agency is supposed to be the biggest big-picture-seer in the place, shouldn't they have seen or realized their officers might be on the decision-making track to make an entire family lay face down on an asphalt parking lot for an extended time in Colorado…in the summer. (Aurora PD) [38]

We seem to have a "lead by example" problem in our profession. This deficiency exists throughout our entire society, not only in law enforcement. The higher the rank or position, the less accountability for anything bad, and the more credit for anything good.

Without going hard on politics, we see it in our government and elected officials. When things go wrong, nobody at the top is responsible. It always falls to some employee who was told to implement the failed program, etc.

Or the CEO that goes from "a rich guy in the world" to "the richest guy in the world", during the year of a worldwide pandemic. Or the "richest guy in the world" who falls to "the second richest guy in the world" during a pandemic. A pandemic which wreaked havoc on their employees and workers, some losing housing and the ability to feed themselves.

And all the while we admonish those workers at the bottom for "not budgeting well" or for "buying too much Starbucks". It seems our society unequivocally rewards and fetes those at the top, and only holds accountable those at the bottom. This attitude must change if we are to improve policing. Sorry, I soapboxed again. Too bad, it's my book.

Waste no more time arguing what a good man should be.

Be one.

-Marcus Aurelius

Model the behavior you wish to see from others.

20: Supervisor Accountability

"Follow My Lead"

Be the Boss

I talked about our SWAT team providing department wide training every summer for active assailant response. The goal was to get all non-SWAT officers on the same page using safer tactics and decision making. We would work on team tactics, less lethal incidents and response, building searching, and shift response to incidents.

The training model was to lay out about five different scenario stations, with different problems or teaching/learning points.

During the first few years, we instructors, individually noticed a similar occurrence. The group's sergeant would assign another officer, usually the newest, to be the "supervisor" in the scenario. This didn't raise flags to us, since we each figured ours' was the only station where they did this during the whole day. It wasn't until, after a year or two of this, that we learned something interesting.

Each group was assigned a new SWAT operator who followed them the entire day. They served as a teacher and explainer in between scenarios. We found the officers would ask them clarification questions they wouldn't ask a veteran operator.

We were debriefing one of our training days, and one of our new operators asked a seemingly innocent question. They asked if the Sgt was supposed to have a different person act as supervisor for all the scenarios. We looked at each other shocked, then quickly understood. Our supervisors were avoiding supervising!

As we talked about this happening at every scenario, we realized the following:

1) The patrol sergeants were not practicing supervising/leading during training.

2) They weren't learning how to supervise/lead critical incidents. This inability regularly showed up in real events.

3) They were afraid of looking like they didn't know what they were doing.

4) They didn't know what they were doing.

The next year we solved that problem. In the lecture portion of the class, then-Sgt Dan Murphy, a SWAT team leader, told his fellow Sgts that they would be in charge of their teams the entire day. They would supervise in every scenario.

We told them it was important they practice supervising events that don't happen every day. We also reminded them this was the perfect place to make mistakes, since nobody would get hurt. This occurrence is indicative of an issue in policing as a whole.

Learn the Job. Really learn the job

We promote supervisors because they pass a test. Depending on the size of the agency, the test can be intensive, or more generic. The applicants may be known by the evaluation panelists, or they may be complete strangers.

The problem comes when people who have qualifications to lead, are unable to pass the tests, while people who can pass tests don't possess or develop the qualities to lead.

I was an FTO (several of my trainees went up the ranks including to the level of deputy chief). I was a public face and representative of the police department. I was picked by my agency to speak on local and nationally syndicated television news shows concerning high profile criminal cases and other law enforcement related topics. But I was not considered promotable, based on the tests.

Toward the end of my career, I went through a couple promotional testing processes. As portfolio experience one may do well with having some supervisory experience on critical incidents.

Obviously, my background was in tactics and critical incident decision making. My sergeant, who I trained when he was in the FTO program as a new officer, used to try to get out of uncomfortable supervision by using a subtle, yet obvious tactic.

During in-progress calls, or calls that might become a large-scale event, my Sgt would come to me and ask if I wanted to handle the tactical response...for my experience for promotion. Seriously.

I had over a decade of tactical experience, including multiple hostage rescues, hundreds of high-risk warrants, and several dozens of barricade operations. I had been shot at more than once and had deployed and applied less lethal munitions against several resistive subjects.

I also regularly served as acting patrol supervisor. I could always use more experience but as far as my agency supervisory experience needs were concerned, I had plenty of it.

The first time he asked, I understood his angle. He was not tactically sound. He knew he was not as confident or competent as me in anything to do with policing, except perhaps taking tests. He was trying to avoid making critical decisions for fear of making a mistake. Scratch that.

He was trying to avoid making critical decisions for fear of looking like he didn't know what he was doing.

The first several times I let him off the hook, because I wanted the situation resolved correctly. People's safety was in jeopardy and I didn't need this Sgt learning at other officers' or citizens' expense.

So, I would say "sounds good", and he would disappear to a safe distance to "supervise the outer perimeter." Kind of like that one lieutenant in the Bastogne episode of "Band of Brothers". Towards the end of my career, I stopped letting him off the hook.

A Supervisor Should Be "Present"

The first time I experienced "supervision by avoidance", I was a three-month SWAT operator. My SWAT pin was still shiny and unscratched.
We were on scene of a suicidal person we dealt with regularly. He had serious mental health issues, but we could always "talk him down". He called saying he had the will and means to force us to kill him.

There was total of 5 officers and one sergeant on the call. I was the less lethal operator on scene with a 37mm less lethal kinetic baton launcher. We called into the open front door of his second-floor apartment for about 45 minutes. We were almost certain he was not inside. An officer who could see into his apartment from another balcony saw no movement the entire time.

As I stood around waiting for a plan to be devised by the Sgt. to finally go in and check for him, the Sgt looked at me and said, "Since you're the SWAT guy, why don't you run this, and I will go around the back with the officer who is back there by himself." I am not the smartest person, but knowing me and knowing him, I knew this option afforded our best chance for success. I agreed, and he was already moving by the time I got out the "K" in "OK'.

...Band of Brothers...

I organized a team, and we went up the stairs to the man's apartment. The K9 officer, who was the lead or point officer, saw the subject lying on the floor with his hands under a pillow looking at us. He gave commands, got no response, then called for less lethal. I moved up and struck the man in his left side with 2 baton rounds. He exhaled forcefully and pulled his hands out and looked away. We took him into custody.

Two days later, my patrol lieutenant, also my SWAT commander, called me into his office. He asked me about the call.

Specifically, he asked me if I thought it was a good idea to have the K9 officer lead the group, since he also deployed the dog inside and had to do double duty. That's a trick question, right?! I didn't think. I knew it was a good idea.

There were three officers going to his apartment, the K9 officer, me, and an officer who had recently finished FTO. By recently, I mean like the week before. I had a less lethal 37 mm baton launcher, so I shouldn't have been first.

The K9 officer had been in 3 shootings to that point. I don't mean, "I thought he had a gun" but it was a hot dog. I mean three, "I'm getting shot at", or "he's running at me swinging a knife in a slashing motion" shootings. Three. And he was still alive, working, and seemingly well adjusted.

My thought was to not require the brand-new officer to make a life and death decision her first week on her own, if I could avoid it. After all, the subject said he had the will and means to force us to kill him. And further (here is where, in retrospect, I believe my career plateaued) I said I would make the same decision again.

As I left the office, I thought about how we got to that talk.

1) The Sgt had a problem with what I did.
2) The Lt. had a problem with what I did.
3) They weren't at the bottom of the stairs, needing to make the decision I had to make.
4) As time went by, I realized why neither of them had been at the bottom of the stairs.
5) As time went by, I wanted to always be "the one at the bottom of the stairs."
6) That was the day I learned about "supervision by avoidance".

In what became a recurring theme in my agency, many supervisors didn't know how to supervise. They knew how to manage, micromanage, and run away, but few knew how to supervise. And by supervise, I mean lead. During my career, I heard a lot of, "Do you think that was a good way to handle that?" or "Why did you do or say that to them?".

They could have just asked me to teach them about good decision making, they didn't have to act like they knew good decision making and were quizzing me about bad decisions after the fact.

We must train our supervisors to be more than managers. They must be leaders. We must train them to not throw their officers to the lions to avoid looking deficient themselves, but to be able to mentor and counsel those officers to success.

What we have today is further evidence of our fear-based training and operation. Out of fear of messing up or looking bad, supervisors don't lead during critical incidents. They don't lead because they never learn how to lead. They don't learn how to fill the role; they learn how to pass the test.

Line officers are left bumbling through critical incidents and out of fear and anxiety, overreact. Afterward, the supervisor sits back and says, "We never trained you to do that." We didn't train them. That's the problem.

Administrators don't require this level of competency from their first line supervisors because they themselves don't possess this knowledge and ability. Think of a professional sports coach who never played the sport at the level they are coaching.

Unless the coach devotes an extraordinary amount of time to learn about the sport at that level, they will never be able to competently teach players to operate at that level. The obstacle is too often ego.

The higher a person gets in a police agency the more they believe that they actually know all the information that exists below them. They think they understand and excel at patrol, traffic, K9, SWAT, narcotics, and every other specialty within the agency.

Except fraud and forgery. Nobody ever thinks they understand that mess. If you even act like you understand fraud and forgery, they make you work it.

If administrators can set aside their egos, they will change the way they manage their resources, and change the way their people will manage resources. By being an example of building confidence through learning, and accepting teaching from others, even subordinates, administrators can change the learning personality of an agency.

They can show that the people with specific knowledge should be listened to. The Subject Matter Experts should be held up as models of the correct ways to do business. It makes no sense to tell someone they are doing something wrong if you cannot then tell them how to do it right.

Recognize Your Agency Subject Matter Experts

We must listen to our Subject Matter Experts (SMEs). Police administrators must require it of their people. Many of the tragedies we have seen in the past several years happened because agencies do not place a premium on the information known by their SMEs.

When we see a botched high-risk narcotic warrant, we usually find it was served by a narcotics team, not a tactical team. This is not to say a tactical team may not subscribe to best practice principles, or they won't come up against a determined suspect.

But tactical teams more typically engage in ongoing, continuous training, constantly evolving decision-making, and use varied resources to solve critical problems. Once we operate outside our area of specialty, we will make mistakes.

Mistakes in policing don't look like burning fries at a burger place. They look like the tragedies in Houston and in Louisville. These two events are prime examples of using antiquated tactics long abandoned by police tactical teams because they violate modern tactical principles. Absent the lying to obtain the warrants, which made the warrants illegal, the tactics used directly contributed to the horrific and avoidable results.

In the Houston warrant, the narcotics team used dynamic movement tactics, overriding and compressing their own OODA loop information processing, while forcing the suspects to do the same.

In the Louisville warrant, detectives declined the offer from the SWAT team to serve the warrant. Based on the information, the SWAT team, the SMEs, said they would have served the warrant during the day not at night.

The risk of not being able to control the situation well because of inherent variables (OODA loop, suspect advantage, space and time, etc.) and the low threat level would have led the SWAT team to serve the warrant at a time when people were awake and better able to process information. Nor would they have performed a no-knock entry.

Suspect advantage undermines no-knock warrants for the simple fact that we must presume the suspect is armed and prepared for our arrival. We are not surprising anyone.

To prevent knee-jerk reactions by either party, SWAT teams are moving away from suddenly surprising dangerous suspects. It just doesn't work how it was drawn up on the white board.

Most tactical teams understand that when we can slow down, and make people aware of our authority and presence, they comply. Very rarely will someone consciously or intentionally get into an armed confrontation with a group of well-armed, highly trained, confident police.

Even the Maricopa, AZ shooting was because they tried to surprise an already armed suspect protecting his home, not because he was trying to shoot it out with police. Once he knew it was the police he gave up.

Because of tragedies, both the cities of Louisville and Houston have banned no-knock warrants completely. The state Kentucky recently moved to ban no-knock exceptions for any warrant. No-knock exceptions have a very limited use in police warrants, but they can be of use. Anytime law enforcement loses a tool, an option, or a resource, we lose our ability to be fully functional and comprehensively successful.

Be careful with your toys…

Suspects will engage police when they perceive an opportunity that they can win and/or get away.

Consider how many times suspects shoot one or two officers, then surrender peacefully to a tactical team. Or the suspect takes their own life when no avenue of escape exists.

In Baton Rouge, LA in April 2020, two officers were ambushed by a murder suspect when they went to "knock and talk" at a home where they believed he was hiding. After killing one officer and wounding the other, the suspect surrendered peacefully when the tactical team arrived.

Logic would argue against the lowkey approach of having two officers attempt to arrest a multiple murder suspect hours after he committed the murders. That should have been a large show of force and superiority. A police officer would still be alive. Zero casualties are acceptable. This was also a violation and disregard of the Safety Priorities.

Law enforcement officers in specialty positions get extra education to understand their craft. They network with other specialists to learn about real incidents and the decisions made, successes had, and lessons learned.

We do this entire profession a disservice by not fully utilizing expertise and holding that advanced knowledge in esteem or high regard. My agency utilized a risk or threat assessment matrix in deciding how or who would serve high risk search and/or arrest warrants. We did this for a few main reasons.

1) Law enforcement officers in specialty positions get extra education to understand their craft. They network with other specialists to learn about real incidents and the decisions made, successes had, and lessons learned.

2) By getting this comprehensive picture we could better decide which tactics would best serve this situation (situation dictates tactics)

3) It increased accountability at the supervisor level throughout our whole agency. All supervisors were required to use this matrix. If something went wrong, their decisions would be judged against the matrix and whether they followed it correctly.

This matrix system worked well, until we discovered some supervisors would omit information in order to prevent their warrant being served by the tactical team. We discovered this "workaround" when a detective told one of our team leaders about a sketchy suspect against whom they served a warrant.

One SWAT team leader filled in the matrix and found this suspect rated a SWAT response. When this was presented to upper administration, they had a fairly typical bureaucratic response. They did little to nothing about it.

Our worry was that our agency would learn the value of our tactical team, SMEs, and our methods for handling high-risk operations only after some of our line officers suffered the tragedies and deaths we saw across the country.

For some supervisors it was a matter of ego. "We are all cops. We can serve warrants too." For us it was a matter of how can we best utilize resources and personnel to keep safe everyone involved?

It always amused me that we were seen as these macho, hyper masculine, "Hut Hut boys" (as one supervisor called us), but we were the ones always working to avoid conflict when resolving critical incidents. Our underlying motto was always, "No news is good news."

Our team's pride was that we would often get questioned by the public, "Why does Fort Collins need a SWAT team? I never knew we had one."

I have been on multiple hostage rescues, over 500 warrants, and been shot at twice, and because of how we resolved critical incidents, except for one of our rescues, we didn't get in the papers. We responded to over 40 incidents per year on average, during my 15 years on the team. The fact that people didn't even know we existed was proof of our low-key resolution ability.

Supervisors must be accountable. They should present the character and qualities they expect from their subordinates. We are having trust issues today in part because supervisors and administrators are failing to prepare their officers to be confident and process information using solid principles and tactics simply because they themselves do not understand these principles.

There is a stronger effort to make excuses post incident, or to hail a fallen officer as a hero when, really, they were part of an easily avoidable mistake that proved fatal to them. Require your agency to listen to the subject matter experts.

They will save lives.

21: Time for action

The police are the public and the public are the police, as Sir Robert Peele said. So, yes, the public is the problem. As a society, we are all complicit in the dysfunction we are experiencing. But the public is also the answer.

Our society only works as a fully functioning organism when we can all interact in a positive way. And law enforcement (LE) only works when we have the trust of the overwhelming majority of the community, not just a small, and shrinking, percentage of people.

Law enforcement must work for everyone, or it works for no one.

While I agree that police officers cannot police with inequity, preference, or partisanship, I understand this is a practiced effort that requires self-awareness, confidence, and discipline.

I would never expect people to not have prejudices (people who say they don t see color or have no prejudices are only kidding themselves). I also think to say "I don't see color" is only possible when you are of the majority population. minorities see color. Too often, the majority population is constantly reminding minorities of their color.

But I do require LEOs to keep their prejudices and biases from negatively impacting their interactions. Because of our role, people who take on the mantle of law enforcement officer must be professional and mature enough to do this. If they are unable, this profession is not for them.

I believe the added component in policing that exacerbates discomfort around color or race, is fear. Fear that is ingrained in LEOs during their training and preparation. Our culturally ingrained fear of the "other" combined with the fear-based police training creates anxious and scared police officers. This is shown in violent actions against innocent people, as well as post incident justifications and rationalizations.

In addition to the extreme events presented earlier, consider the following events from the past few years.

1) A Tulsa, OK police officer, one in a group of 4 officers, shot Terence Crutcher as Crutcher stood next to his SUV, arms raised as commanded to do so. The officer later said she had "never been so scared in her life."

2) A Salt Lake City, UT officer shot and killed a homeless man who was stopped for riding a bicycle at night with no light. He was found to have a warrant and decided to flee. As the suspect ran *away* from the officers, he produced a knife, possibly to get rid of it. One officer deployed a taser, as another officer fired his weapon. The shooting officer said that even having served two combat tours in Iraq he "had never been so scared as I was in that moment."

3) Kawaski Trawick, a New York City fitness instructor with a history of mental health issues, was shot and killed by a police officer who had been called to a mental health check on Trawick. The entire episode from contact to killing lasted less than 2 minutes. As Trawick repeatedly asked why the police were in his house, neither officer answered his question, but merely yelled over and over for him to drop the bread knife he was already holding when they opened his front door.

We have literally made fear the primary and acceptable reason police use lethal force against people. The canned response for officers, is the trite cliché, "I was in fear for my life."

This is the mantra police memorize to excuse, justify, rationalize, or absolve them for any and all use of lethal force. How can we be so highly trained, so well-equipped yet so scared and panicked all the time?

We allow and encourage fear to play too large a part in law enforcement tactics and decision making. We must change how we do business. We officers need to see ourselves differently. We need to alter and rethink our perception, "I am the most important always".

LEOs need to train to be confident, not scared. We can be scared without any training. It's cheaper and takes less time to become proficient.

Police are self-proclaimed highly trained professionals. We should use force as a conditioned, practiced, reasoned response, not a knee-jerk panicked, fear reaction. Rather than excusing the use of lethal force because “I was in fear for my life”, a better explanation might be, “I used lethal force because the situation dictated that any lesser force would not have been sufficient to save the victim, or myself.”

We can prepare, train, and support our officers to move into a new era of policing. A new model of public safety. We are the sheepdogs, but the flock doesn’t recognize us anymore. We have spent too much time away from the flock chasing wolves. We have become dangerous to them. They want us to go away.

Law enforcement must reconnect, first on a basic human level, then on a partnership level. We cannot continue to place blame for the condition of our situation at anyone else’s feet. We have been doing that too long and it is only making the situation worse.

It is time to take responsibility for the problem. Even if we didn’t start it, and we don’t feel we contribute to it, own the problem. The only way to fix something broken is to take responsibility for its welfare and repair. We are wasting precious time trying to ignore the problem and make someone else responsible for it. Law enforcement has to do some soul searching and introspection.

This profession cannot continue to claim an “untarnished badge” as those among our ranks plant evidence on dozens of motorists to boost statistics, or "railroad" local minorities into jail (both travesties happened in Florida within the past three years).

We cannot claim we are accountable, as officers shoot unarmed, nonthreatening, innocent citizens and suffer no consequences.

We cannot proclaim our trustworthiness as more and more prisoners' cases are overturned because of perjured officer testimony, or body worn camera and citizen video contradicts officer statements in use of force situations.

Law enforcement has a fantastic opportunity right now. The community is hungry for a new way to view police. They want to feel safe, protected, and valued. They want a partnership with law enforcement. As much as a negative atmosphere has descended on our society like fog over the airport, people still look forward to clearing skies.

Our communities still want a positive and trusting relationship with LEOs. We can do our part to restore that trust, that positive image. No, it will never be 100%. We aren't firefighters. But we can increase the numbers.

There those who seek to abolish policing and want to believe we could all live together in harmony without law enforcement and enforcers. But a heterogenous society, like the United States, needs an entity that serves as a rudder to steer people back to what is acceptable to the society as a whole. We need people who act as our "better angels".

Let's provide law enforcement officers with mindset shifts and training changes they can make themselves or can be implemented without an organization wide effort. These changes can be small, easy to do, and incremental in scope. If shifts are too big or seem too large, they become unmanageable. People see more obstacles than clear paths.

The most lasting changes occur in small increments. Everything I have presented in this book can be taken on in pieces, beginning with mindset and self-understanding, moving through to tactical decision-making and scenario-based training. Implemented slowly and with intent to promote change.

Please take the time to process new information in this book. It was written using many different thought perspectives. This is not a one-dimensional book; it draws from varied subjects as different as can be from typical law enforcement. I include everything from teachings from religion and ancient roman philosophy to modern business practices to 100-year-old Japanese Psychotherapy.

I believe police officers must be as comprehensive as possible in their knowledge and education. We work with people. And the ability to be competent at our work depends on a broad base of understanding. We must understand the what, where, when, and how of our decision-making. And we need to know the glue that holds everything together and determines the rest; the WHY. I say a police officer must have knowledge a mile wide and an inch deep. Maybe even 6 inches deep.

The focus of this book is on improving service and public trust through improved preparation and training. This book is about police reform in a specific area. This is not an exhaustive work.

For a much more comprehensive coverage of policing reform issues I suggest a great book written by a fellow retired police officer from Connecticut. Captain Lawrence Hunter (retired) recently published his book on Police Reform. I will list it in the Glossary.

The only group police can control in the broken relationship is themselves. And a critical area in need of improvement is in police mindset and training.

I think that if we can change this area, we will go far in solving many of the "action" problems. If we can build confidence and not fear, our officers will first see themselves differently, and then see others differently. And in this case, different is good.

Seeing people differently means LEOs not seeing everyone as an equal threat. Or not as any threat at all. We can prevent many of the tragedies we are experiencing just by changing our view of ourselves.

All change happens within. We don't change our own world by changing everyone else in it. If you move your house, all you have done is change the scenery. The structure is still the same. We want to remodel the house.

Society needs law enforcement. We need normal citizens who will assume the role of guardian in the public safety arena and help maintain our quality of life.

This book is another component in the machine that will bring about effective, lasting, and positive police reform. The work will take effort. It will not be easy. It took generations to get here, it will take generations to get out. But the effort is worth it. The public is worth it. Law enforcement officers are worth it.

People are worth it.

End Notes/References

[1]https://en.wikipedia.org/wiki/Robert_Peel

[2]https://5315b3c7-4fd2-421c-be7a-cbaa4348a7c2.filesusr.com/ugd/b44013_086d65c1284b4734b7fdce4532edf02a.pdf

[3]https://nypost.com/2020/06/08/trump-we-wont-be-dismantling-police-99-percent-are-great-people/

[4]https://www.cnn.com/videos/us/2017/06/22/philando-castile-facebook-and-dashcam-full-mashup-video-ctn.cnn

[5]https://www.facebook.com/michiganfop/posts/sheriff-d-clarke-says-it-bestits-not-the-police-who-need-to-be-retrained-its-the/3018437184899889/

[6]https://nypost.com/2020/12/08/video-shows-fatal-police-shooting-of-kawaski-trawick/

[7]http://nleomf.org/wp-content/uploads/2021/01/2020-LE-Officers-Fatalities-Report-opt.pdf

[8]https://oklahoman.com/article/5678318/man-killed-by-police-stabbed-a-letter-carrier-in-2014-authorities-said

[9]https://www.cnn.com/2020/10/06/us/jonathan-price-police-shooting-texas/index.html

[10]**https://www.bbc.com/news/stories-53052917**

[11] *Nonsense, The Power of Not Knowing*, Jamie Holmes, 2015, Broadway Books.
[12]https://www.cnn.com/2020/11/16/politics/hate-crimes-fbi-report/index.html

[13]**https://www.history.com/topics/reconstruction/ku-klux-klan**

[14] **https://data.census.gov**

[15]https://www.rev.com/blog/transcripts/ny-police-union-chief-speech-transcript-stop-treating-us-like-animals

[16] **https://nleomf.org/facts-figures/law-enforcement-facts**

[17] Source: **www.Sportrac.com**

[18]https://www.forbes.com/sites/andrewdepietro/2020/04/23/police-officer-salary-state/?sh=52a375dc2010

[19]https://www.vox.com/identities/2017/5/30/15713254/cleveland-police-tamir-rice-timothy-loehmann

[20] Breonna Taylor killing

[21]**https://www.washingtonpost.com/nation/2019/08/09/amir-worship-chicago-swat-raid-knee-lawsuit/**

[22]**https://www.nbcnews.com/news/us-news/mississippi-police-fatally-shoot-man-wrong-house-while-serving-warrant-n786681**

[23]**https://chicago.cbslocal.com/2020/12/17/you-have-the-wrong-place-body-camera-video-shows-moments-police-handcuff-innocent-naked-woman-during-wrong-raid/**

[24]**https://www.cbsnews.com/news/andre-hill-shooting-officer-no-threat/**

[25]**https://www.cnn.com/2016/09/20/us/oklahoma-tulsa-police-shooting/index.html**

[26] **https://www.bbc.com/news/stories-53052917**

[27] *On Combat,* Lt. Colonel Dave Grossman with Loren W. Christensen, 2008 Warrior Science Publications, Third Edition

[28] Captain Hunter's Podcast on Pod bean, Apple, and other services.

[29] *Values for a New Millennium,* Robert L. Humphrey, J. D., second printing 2005 The Life Values Press

[30] https://www.police1.com/legal/articles/how-to-avoid-legal-missteps-on-suicidal-subject-calls-HkougftJBdMo1sto/

[31] Source, **www.weather.com**

[32]**https://oklahoman.com/article/5678388/a-black-man-killed-by-okc-police-had-severe-mental-illness-the-officers-on-paid-leave-had-no-crisis-intervention-training**

[33] **https://www.youtube.com/watch?v=jQvDn9MEtNo**

[34] 1983, MGM, Bob Clark Director

[35]**https://www.vox.com/identities/2017/5/30/15713254/cleveland-police-tamir-rice-timothy-loehmann**

[36]**https://www.justice.gov/sites/default/files/opa/press-releases/attachments/2014/12/04/cleveland_division_of_polic e_findings_letter.pdf**

[37] *Psycho-Cybernetics,* by Maltz, Maxwell, MD, FCIS 2015 Psycho-Cybernetics Foundation

[38]**https://www.foxnews.com/us/colorado-aurora-police-draw-guns-handcuff-black-girls**

Glossary

Accommodate–Open your frame of understanding to accept new and different information. This is how we grow our knowledge.

Assimilation–Try to make new information conform to previously held beliefs and knowledge. This is how we limit our ability to grow intellectually.

Body Worn Camera-BWC–The camera system many agencies now employ. It is typically a square camera worn on the front of the officer's uniform. There are versions where a camera is mounted in glasses worn by the officer.

Close Quarters Battle-CQB–This is the name given to military movement and tactics for engaging enemy combatants.

Criticize–Pointing out another's mistakes or performance deficiencies with the intent to cause pain and suffering.

Critique–Pointing out another's mistakes or performance deficiencies with the intent to improve their performance and encourage learning.

District Attorney-DA–The prosecuting attorney for a county and district court.

Distraction Device–A light, sound, heat, and air pressure producing tool that, in size only, resembles a grenade. A distraction device does not fragment like a grenade. Nor does it explode like a high explosive or bomb. It is merely meant to upset a person's information processing loop, OODA loop, and give them a moment to pause.

Distraction devices are not intended nor are they manufactured to give people permanent hearing, vision, or other physiological damage. Some are considered a low explosive, while others operate by electrical or other means.

Fear-based police training–A method of training police officers where everyone they come across is likely to be a threat. Not a possible threat, a likely threat. It seeks to increase officer safety by making them distrust all strangers. This is reinforced through no-win training where officers get "killed" in scenarios unless they are aggressive and strike first.

Flash-bang–A Distraction Device. Also called Flash Sound Distraction Device, Noise Flash Distraction Device, and similar.

Jerrod Hardy, Team Hardy, teamhardy.net–police trainer, retired police officer, author.

Hunter, Lawrence–Police Reform: A Retired Police Captain's Perspective on the Evolution of Law Enforcement in America & How to Improve the Criminal Justice System 2020

LEO–Law Enforcement Officer

Line of Duty Death-LODD–This is the classification whenever an officer dies while on duty, in any manner. This includes anything from felonious murder to 9/11 related illnesses and heart attacks. In 2020, COVID 19 was responsible for more officer deaths than all other manners combined.

No-Knock Warrant-The "no-knock' is an exception to a normal warrant. It is meant to allow the police to make entry without giving the occupant of the residence an advanced notice prior to entry. The intent was to prevent the occupant/suspect from either arming themselves or destroying evidence (typically narcotics).

The no-knock exception operates under an antiquated mindset and violates many contemporary concepts and principles that are the foundation of police tactical decision making. No-knock exceptions should be used extremely sparingly.

OIS-Officer-Involved Shooting.

OODA Loop-information processing loop. How we do everything.

Physical Training-PT-Calisthenics, exercise.

PTSD-Post Traumatic Stress Disorder

Scenario Based Training-SBT-The use of role players and role playing to provide a realistic training and decision-making situation. The officer interacts with people pretending to be any other person in the scenario. This allows officers to interact with real people, under stress, without the fear of real injury or even the possibility of making mistakes.

Sir Robert Peel-Credited with developing modern policing. He created the London Metropolitan Police in 1829. His direction led to science-backed criminal investigations and the development of crime scene processing to solve crimes where the suspect was not located or identified at the scene.

Taser–An electronic restraining device that fires to metal barbs attached to various length copper wires. An electric current at high milliamperage, but low voltage, creates an instant muscle cramping intended to incapacitate a person. The electric cycle lasts 5 seconds. The person will not lose consciousness, not get "knocked out" as is commonly depicted in movies. The incapacitation is temporary, and pain is not felt beyond the actual electrical shock.

Acknowledgements

I want to acknowledge many people for giving me the knowledge, the passion, the understanding, and desire to put down these words. I cannot name every one of them. Some of my best teachers are people whose names have been lost to time or never known but crossed my path during the 53 years I have wandered this earth.

I want to recognize my partner in life, Alice Duncan. Her presence, energy, being has supported and sustained me at times when my self-confidence was nonexistent. It has been her wisdom and holistic nurturing that has helped me develop who I am today. And I could just sit and look at her all day.

There have been many people who have helped me in my development as a person, father, Guardian, and trainer. My mentors of my youth, Bruce Nelson and Jim Ruane, my track and football coaches, respectively. Both men gave me life lessons that have long outlasted the athletic lessons they taught me that led to high school accolades and a college football scholarship. They were true role models of character and integrity.

Dan Murphy, Marcus Hopkins, Doug. Smith, and the other members of my SWAT team. Dan gave me the support to develop my tactical acumen, as well as my teaching credentials. He is one of those unicorns in law enforcement, a true leader.

Marcus, Doug, and I were the nucleus of an extremely competent tactical team for over a decade. A team that provided safety and security for our community that was second to none.

Our 7 children, and for now, 8 grandchildren. My kids have been my teachers more than I have been theirs. Their accomplishments moved me to create this book. The future safety of my little brown grandchildren has been a prime motivating factor for me to help improve police performance.

I want to acknowledge my mother, Vera Neal. She was my first example of unselfish sacrifice for others. I thank the universe every day for my life coming through her. Her time was cut shorter than I would ever want, but I am happy and grateful for the experience I had as her son.

About the Author

Marc Neal Marc has been a nationally recognized police tactics
trainer since 2005. He has taught in almost every state in the US
and in the United Arab Emirates. In the past 15 years, he has worked with over 1500 officers from the US and over a dozen foreign countries.

He retired from law enforcement after 20 years in both detention and municipal policing, spending 15 years as a member of a Special Weapons and Tactics team. Marc worked 9 years as a detective and has been interviewed about cases on nationally syndicated television programs.

During his tenure, he served as entry, point operator, explosive breacher, and team leader. Marc was involved in numerous hostage rescues, including a vehicle rescue.

Marc helped establish his agency's diversity program and continues to teach police diversity and anti-bias courses in addition to tactics, through his company, ONYX Training Group.

Marc was born and raised in San Francisco, CA. He has lived in Colorado since 1992 and now lives in downtown Denver. Marc and his wife Ali Duncan have 7 children and 8 grandchildren scattered around the world.

Marc can be reached at mneal@onyxtg.com

Made in the USA
Columbia, SC
03 June 2021